How To Be A More Effective Church Leader

A Special Edition for Pastors and Other Church Leaders

NORMAN SHAWCHUCK

SPIRITUAL GROWTH RESOURCES®

How To
Be a More Effective Church Leader
Copyright © 1981 by Norman Shawchuck, Ph.D

> This edition is designed especially for, and dedicated to,
> busy pastors and church leaders everywhere.
> They hold the most demanding leadership positions in the world.

Printed in the United States of America
Eighth Printing: 2000

Published by:

SPIRITUAL GROWTH RESOURCES®
A Division of Organization Resources Press

Follow These Steps to Become
A More Effective Leader

Just before you begin your study, why not pause a moment to ask God for wisdom to aid in your learning and application of the new leadership discoveries you are about to make?

"If any of you lacks wisdom
Ask God
Who gives to all generously
And it will be given . . ."

James 1:5

"Wisdom from above
is first pure,
then peaceable,
gentle,
open to reason,
full of mercy,
and good fruits . . ."

James 3:17

"Teach me wisdom
in my inner heart . . ."

Psalms 51:6

A DEFINITION OF LEADERSHIP

As a busy leader you are responsible for many programs and activities. There is always more to do than you can possibly accomplish alone. Therefore, you must often rely upon others to carry out the programs and activities for which you share major responsibility. You want to be successful and effective in your work, yet much of this is dependent upon the cooperation and support of the persons with whom you work.

LEADERSHIP

Carrying responsibility for the success of an organization's programs, coupled with the need to depend on the cooperation and performance of other persons for carrying out those programs, often causes a leader more than a little bit of concern. The leader often wonders, "Am I pushing too much, or not enough?" "How might I best be able to motivate these people?" "What is the most effective way to work with this group?"

These and other questions are the constant concern of persons in leadership positions. To be effective a leader must understand his/her leadership behavior and how it affects the persons he/she wants to lead.

The leader, however, is not the only source of influence upon members of the group. Other influences, such as family, job, relationships, events in society are only a few of the many other items which influence, for good or ill, the behavior of individual group members and the situation in which the group carries out its work. With all of this in mind, leadership can be described as a *function* of the *leader*, the *followers*, and other *situational* variables. This concept of leadership can be formulated as follows:[1] L = f(l,f,s) or leadership equals the function of the leader, the followers and the situation.

Many definitions have been given for leadership. One which I use most often is, "Leadership is the process of influencing the activities of an individual or group in efforts toward accomplishing goals in a given situation. Roy Clifford and Jerry Robinson describe leadership as "A learned behavioral skill which includes the ability to help others achieve their potential as individuals and team members."[2]

George R. Terry states, "Leadership is the activity of influencing people to strive willingly for group objectives." Robert Tannenbaum, Irving Weschler, and Fred Massarik, define leadership as "Interpersonal influence exercised in a situation and directed, through the communication process, toward the attainment of a special goal or goals."[3]

From the many definitions of leadership, two elements keep emerging: leadership is both an *ability* and an *activity*. Leadership is comprised of qualities and of skills in the leader's actions and behaviors that cause people to respond. Hence a simple definition of leadership; *leadership is the ability, and the activity of influencing people, and of shaping their behavior.*

Anytime someone attempts to influence the behavior of another person or of a group, regardless of the reason, leadership is being exercised. The motive or reason may be entirely within the leader or it may be shared by the group or individual being influenced.

MANAGEMENT

One way to define the difference between leadership and management is to say that management is a specific kind of leadership. All management is leadership, but not all leadership is management. Management does what leadership does but its focus is upon accomplishing common purposes and goals within an organizational setting. Hence, *management is the ability and activity of influencing people and shaping their behavior to accomplish goals within an organization.*

Management and leadership are related but not the same. All managers must lead but not all leaders manage within organizations. A leader may be working to attain his/her own goals but a manager must be working to attain organizational goals. The organization may be a business, a school, a church, a hospital or even a family. The key idea is that the purposes or goals of this group are shared in com-

[1]Hersey, Paul and Kenneth H. Blanchard, *Management of Organizational Behavior*, Third Edition (Englewood Cliffs, NJ: Prentice-Hall, 1977), p. 84.

[2]Robinson, Jerry and Roy Clifford, *Leadership Roles in Community Groups* (Urbana, IL: College of Agriculture, University of Illinois at Urbana-Champaign, 1975) p. 2.

[3]Hersey, Paul and Kenneth H. Blanchard, *Management of Organizational Behavior*, p. 84.

mon. Management then, is leadership exercised to accomplish those shared objectives and purposes.

Leaders can be charismatic, great visionaries, attracting followers with the power of their own personality or ideas. Some of the greatest events and movements in history were caused by inspiring leaders who were able to move people to new behaviors or ideas by sharing their vision. Managers, on the other hand, work to accomplish a goal or vision that has emerged from within the group or the organization it serves.

The organization exists as a method for accomplishing common goals, and management serves that organization. In order to achieve its purposes, the organization relies upon five specific management functions:

1. Assessing problems and opportunities

2. Goal setting

3. Planning to achieve goals

4. Implementing the plans

5. Evaluating the organization's effectiveness

In addition to the five basic managerial functions, three levels of skills have been identified as necessary for the process of management.[4] They are technical skills, human skills and conceptual skills:

Technical Skills: The knowledge, methods, techniques, training and experience necessary to perform a specific task.

Human Skills: The ability to work with and through people, to be able to understand and motivate people.

Conceptual Skills: To understand the organization as a whole, to see where one's activity fits into the overall organization, to be able to articulate the purposes of the organization and to act according to those purposes.

Whereas human skills are necessary for all levels of management, the mix of technical and conceptional skills vary according to the level of management.

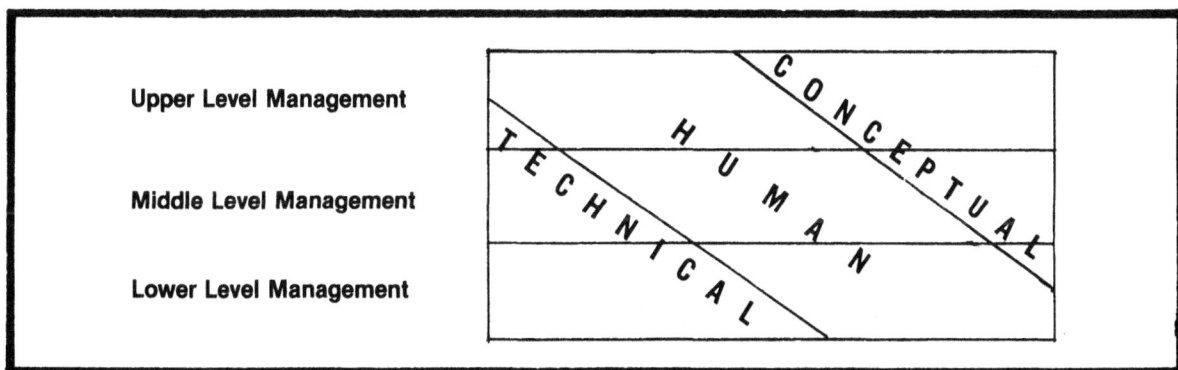

Figure 1.1

[4]Hersey, Paul and Kenneth H. Blanchard, *Management of Organizational Behavior*, pp. 6 and 7.

Whenever you attempt to influence the behavior of another person you are exercising leadership. By virtue of your job or position, you may be a formal leader, and if you exercise this leadership within an organization you are, by definition, a manager.

Step 2 of this manual will allow you to take a survey of your own leadership behavior to assist you in:

- identifying the type of leader you are
- recognizing your range of leadership styles and behavior
- understanding and assessing a group's effectiveness
- choosing the leadership style which would be most appropriate and effective with a particular group.[5]

---

[5] Major pieces of this step were written by Dr. R. George Sarauskas.

A SURVEY OF
YOUR LEADERSHIP STYLES

to enable you to identify the way you
generally respond to various
leadership situations

Approximate time needed to complete the survey: 25 minutes . . .

HOW TO PROCEED . . .

PLEASE READ CAREFULLY:

In your organization you are the leader of a committee, group, or department which is responsible for a significant program. Your group must meet regularly to make decisions. In addition, all group members must assume responsibilities for carrying out the decisions.

Following are twelve situations which you encounter during your time as the group's leader. For each situation you have six possible behavioral responses. Please study each situation and the possible behavioral responses carefully, then CIRCLE THE LETTER OF THE RESPONSE which you think would most closely describe your behavioral response to the situation.

As you complete the SURVEY, please remember this is NOT a test. There are no right or wrong responses. The SURVEY will be helpful to you only to the extent that you circle the responses which would be most characteristic of your leadership behavior.

CIRCLE ONLY ONE CHOICE FOR EACH SITUATION!

SITUATION NO. 1:

YOU HAVE BEEN PROVIDING THE GROUP WITH SOCIO-EMOTIONAL SUPPORT, BUT LITTLE DIRECTION. RELATIONSHIPS AND EFFECTIVENESS ARE VERY GOOD. MEMBERS HAVE SUGGESTIONS FOR NEEDED PROGRAM CHANGES.

You Would: *(Circle one)*

A. Allow the group to plan the change, remaining available for consultation.

B. Plan the change strategy, giving clear assignments.

C. Allow the group to plan the change, then carry it out for them.

D. Implement necessary changes, incorporating group recommendations.

E. Allow the group to plan and implement the change on its own.

F. Instruct the group that no program is ever perfect, present specific strategy, and assign responsibilities for implementation.

SITUATION NO. 2:

YOUR HIGHLY EFFECTIVE GROUP HAS BEEN ALMOST ENTIRELY SELF-DIRECTED. NOW, HOWEVER, IT IS HAVING DIFFICULTY CARRYING OUT ITS PRESENT ASSIGNMENT.

You Would: *(Circle one)*

A. Carry out the assignment for them.

B. Leave the group free to work it out as they see fit.

C. Give specific step-by-step instructions for carrying out the assignment.

D. Encourage the group to continue working on the assignment, remaining available for consultation.

E. Decide what has gone wrong with the group to cause this sudden ineffectiveness, and correct it.

F. Give instructions for carrying out the assignment, incorporating group suggestions.

SITUATION NO. 3:

YOU HAVE BEEN FRIENDLY AND SUPPORTIVE OF THE GROUP'S GOALS AND IDEAS. RELATIONSHIPS ARE GOOD; HOWEVER, USUAL EFFECTIVENESS IS BEGINNING TO DECLINE.

You Would: *(Circle one)*

A. Present new procedures, emphasizing the need for following them closely.

B. Encourage the group to formulate plans for improving effectiveness, remaining available for consultation.

C. Share your observations with the group, inviting suggestions for improving effectiveness.

D. Do nothing until it became clear whether effectiveness would improve or continue to decline.

E. Do more of the group's work yourself.

F. Specify and enforce procedures. Do much of the work yourself.

SITUATION NO. 4:

YOU ARE THE NEW LEADER OF A VERY INEFFECTIVE GROUP. THERE IS MUCH TASK CONFUSION AND RELATIONSHIPS ARE POOR. THE PREVIOUS LEADER WAS UNINVOLVED IN THE GROUP'S AFFAIRS.

You Would: *(Circle one)*

A. Begin providing more structure and direction, encouraging group recommendations.

B. Do the group's work yourself until you were able to find out what is wrong with the group, and correct it.

C. Allow the group to chart its own course.

D. Define the task, give specific assignments, and check on follow-through.

E. Do the group's work yourself.

F. Encourage the group to formulate plans for improving effectiveness, remaining available for consultation.

SITUATION NO. 5:

YOUR GROUP HAS JUST COMPLETED A LONG-RANGE PLANNING PROCESS AND IS NOW READY TO PUT THEIR PLANS INTO ACTION. YOU WERE ALMOST ENTIRELY UNINVOLVED IN THE PLANNING.

You Would: *(Circle one)*

A. Allow the group to implement plans on its own.

B. Encourage the group to implement its plans, remaining available for consultation.

C. Initiate and direct implementation procedures, incorporating group recommendations.

D. Remind them that most groups make plans but few ever carry them out. Give specific implementation procedures, doing everything you could personally to carry them out.

E. Implement the plans by defining roles and assigning responsibilities.

F. Wait until the group has formulated implementation procedures, then do whatever you could to carry them out.

SITUATION NO. 6:

THE GROUP HAS GROWN TO BE QUITE EFFECTIVE AND RELATIONSHIPS ARE GOOD. YOU HAVE BEEN PROVIDING SOCIO-EMOTIONAL SUPPORT, BUT FEEL YOU MAY NOT BE GIVING THE GROUP AS MUCH DIRECTION AS YOU SHOULD.

You Would: *(Circle one)*

A. Inform the group you are feeling guilty about your lack of involvement and begin to exercise control of decision-making and assignments.

B. Discuss your feelings with the group and begin to provide more structure and direction.

C. Exercise more control by specifying procedures and responsibilities.

D. Continue to play a friendly supportive role.

E. Begin doing as much of their detail work as you could.

F. Leave the group free to provide for its own support and direction.

SITUATION NO. 7:

RELATIONSHIPS AND EFFECTIVENESS ARE IMPROVING STEADILY. YOU HAVE BEEN INTERPRETING THE TASK AND GIVING EXPLICIT INSTRUCTIONS FOR CARRYING IT OUT.

You Would: *(Circle one)*

A. Turn planning and decision-making over to the group, remaining available for consultation.

B. Do as much of the group's work as possible.

C. Remind the group it is still far from perfect. Outline specific steps for improvement, and do more work yourself.

D. Emphasize the importance of their work and have other assignments laid out when current tasks are completed.

E. Continue to press for increased effectiveness while allowing the group more to say in defining and planning the task.

F. Allow the group to chart its own course.

SITUATION NO. 8:

PREVIOUS GROUP RELATIONSHIPS AND EFFECTIVENESS WERE POOR. BY GIVING CLEAR ASSIGNMENTS AND CHECKING ON FOLLOW-THROUGH, BOTH ARE IMPROVING. NOW, HOWEVER, THE GROUP IS CONFUSED OVER A REQUIREMENT TO SUBMIT A 20% REDUCED BUDGET WITHIN TWO WEEKS.

You Would: *(Circle one)*

A. Leave the group alone to do the necessary budget planning.

B. Implement necessary procedures, incorporating group recommendations.

C. Inform the group you are as confused as they, and prepare the budget for them.

D. Prepare the new budget for them.

E. Encourage the group to revise its budget, being careful not to hurt leader-member relationships.

F. Define the task and give explicit steps for carrying it out.

SITUATION NO. 9:

YOU HAVE JUST BEEN APPOINTED THE LEADER OF A GROUP WITH AN EXCELLENT RECORD OF EFFECTIVENESS AND RELATIONSHIPS. THE PREVIOUS LEADER WAS RELATIVELY UNINVOLVED IN GROUP AFFAIRS.

You Would: *(Circle one)*

A. Define new roles and responsibilities, and make specific assignments.

B. Do all of the group's work you possibly could.

C. Encourage the group to continue operating as previously, being careful not to damage new leader-group relationships.

D. Allow the group to function as before.

E. Inform them you feel unworthy to lead such an effective group, and ask for full support. Assign new roles and responsibilities.

F. Talk it over with the group, then assign new roles and responsibilities.

SITUATION NO. 10:

YOUR GROUP HAS A LONG RECORD OF EFFECTIVENESS. INTERPERSONAL RELATIONSHIPS HAVE BEEN GOOD. IT HAS NOT BEEN NECESSARY FOR YOU TO BE CONCERNED ABOUT GIVING SUPPORT OR DIRECTION. NOW, SERIOUS CONFLICT HAS DEVELOPED WITHIN THE GROUP. DIFFERING MEMBERS HAVE BROKEN OFF RELATIONSHIPS.

You Would: *(Circle one)*

    A. Bring the group together and suggest a solution to the conflict.

    B. Do nothing.

    C. Impose rules for resolving the conflict, and check on follow-through.

    D. Inform the group such behavior is immature. Outline specific steps for resolving the conflict.

    E. Encourage members to resolve the conflict, being careful not to hurt leader-member relationships.

    F. Ask the differing sides what you might do to correct the problem, and do what they suggest.

SITUATION NO. 11:

YOU HAVE BEEN GIVING EXPLICIT INSTRUCTIONS AND CHECKING ON FOLLOW-THROUGH. THE GROUP HAS GROWN IN MATURITY. NOW, HOWEVER, EFFECTIVENESS IS DECLINING AND MEMBERS SEEM TO BE QUESTIONING YOUR AUTHORITARIAN LEADERSHIP.

You Would: *(Circle one)*

    A. Let the group know your disappointment regarding their attitude, and set a good example by doing all the work you possibly could.

    B. Allow the group to function on its own.

    C. Encourage the group to assume more responsibility for its affairs, remaining available for consultation.

    D. Personally take care of important tasks.

    E. Give less explicit instructions, but continue to check on follow-through.

    F. Emphasize the importance of the task, and give specific assignments. Check on follow-through.

SITUATION NO. 12:

YOUR GROUP HAS SEVERAL NEWLY APPOINTED WILLING, BUT INEXPERIENCED, MEMBERS. YOU MUST NOW INSTALL NEW ORGANIZATIONAL POLICIES.

You Would: *(Circle one)*

    A. Inform the group your role is to serve them. Demonstrate this by implementing new policies on your own.

    B. Inform them the new policies are complex and, to make it easier for them, assign their roles and responsibilities and do most of the work yourself.

    C. Allow the group to implement policies on its own.

    D. Incorporate group recommendations into your plans for initiating new policies.

    E. Define the task, assign specific roles and responsibilities, and check on follow-through.

    F. Encourage the group to define its task and to assign roles and responsibilities, being careful not to hurt leader-member relationships.

YOU HAVE COMPLETED THE

SURVEY AND ARE NOW READY TO

DETERMINE THE RESULTS

Beyond this page awaits for you some important discoveries regarding your own leadership and ability to provide a group with the type of leadership it needs. In addition, there are insights into effective leadership practice. Learning and applying these concepts is certain to enhance your leadership and its results.

PLEASE TURN THE PAGE ————————————————➤
AND PROCEED TO SCORE THE SURVEY

Notice

For your own insight and learning it is imperative that you complete and score the SURVEY before reading Steps 3-7. Please complete the SURVEY before reading beyond this point.

HOW TO SCORE THE SURVEY OF YOUR LEADERSHIP STYLES ...

I. Order and Range of Style Preferences

1. ON FIGURE 2.1, circle the same letter for each <u>situation</u> that you circled in your survey. (This designates the LEADERSHIP STYLE you chose for each situation.)

2. TOTAL the number of choices (circles) for each LEADERSHIP STYLE and enter subtotals in the spaces provided for these SCORES.

3. Transfer these scores onto the SCORE column of FIGURE 2.2 in descending order of magnitude.

4. List the corresponding style names (FIGURE 2.2) in the STYLE column.

FIGURE 2.2 now provides you with two important insights into your leadership behavior:

1. A rank ordering of your LEADERSHIP STYLES PREFERENCES. The style receiving the highest score is the style you prefer most, etc.

2. The RANGE OF STYLES, or number of styles, you are able and/or willing to utilize.

These two pieces of information say something about your general philosophy and orientation toward leadership. For example, the style receiving the highest score will tend to be your preferred style of leadership; the style you feel most comfortable with and will use most often. The style receiving the second highest score will tend to be the style you will "fall back on" when for some reason your preferred style does not produce the results you expect, and you decide you must change your approach, etc.

The number of times you chose each style suggests the strength of preference you give to each style.

The scoring used in this survey is based upon leadership theories developed by Ohio State Leadership Studies; Blake and Mouton, Managerial Grid; Hersey and Blanchard, Tri-Dimensional Leader Effectiveness Model.

ORDER OF YOUR STYLE PREFERENCES		
Choice	**Style**	**Score**
1st.		
2nd.		
3rd.		
4th.		
5th.		
6th.		

Figure 2.2

Leadership Styles	Situations												Number of Choices
	1	**2**	**3**	**4**	**5**	**6**	**7**	**8**	**9**	**10**	**11**	**12**	
Task Oriented	B	C	A	D	E	C	D	F	A	C	F	E	
Total Involvement	D	F	C	A	C	B	E	B	F	A	E	D	
Person Oriented	A	D	B	F	B	D	A	E	C	E	C	F	
Passive Involvement	E	B	D	C	A	F	F	A	D	B	B	C	
Slave	C	A	E	E	F	E	B	D	B	F	D	A	
Martyr	F	E	F	B	D	A	C	C	E	D	A	B	

Figure 2.1

- 16 -

INTERPRETING YOUR SCORES

PREFERRED AND BACK-UP STYLES

The number of times you chose to use each style in response to the twelve situations indicates your preferred style (the one you choose most often), plus your back-up styles (those which you "fall back on" when for some reason your earlier leadership behavior is not producing your intended results). You will tend to enter every leadership situation with your preferred style and remain there until you become convinced it is not working satisfactorily, at which time you will fall back on your second style preference. If this does not work, you will utilize your third preference, etc.

The number of times you selected a style in response to each of the twelve situations indicates the degree of preference, or the strength, you give to that style. **A style must have been selected in response to at least two of the situations to be considered a back-up style.** All of the styles, then, with a score of two or more, make up your STYLE RANGE. If you selected only one or two styles two or more times, you perceive of yourself as having a limited range of leadership behaviors. If you selected three or four of the styles two or more times, you perceive of yourself as having a wide range of leadership behaviors.

NOTE: As you now proceed to learn the meaning of the various leadership styles, please keep these most important principles in mind:

1. Leadership styles are learned, therefore, you can learn new ones, discard others, etc.

2. There is no "ideal" leadership style, rather each style, with the exception of slave and martyr, is more effective in certain situations and less effective in others.

3. Group leadership needs vary, therefore, one group may need a certain leadership style while another may need a different style.

4. Finally, whatever score you achieved in the survey is not the most important consideration. It is more important that you go on from this point to learn and use effective leadership styles tailored to the needs of the groups and persons you lead.

THE LEADERSHIP STYLES DESCRIBED

Leadership is a "process of influencing the activities of an individual or group in efforts toward accomplishing goals in a given situation."[1] We are all, therefore, leaders in many situations; as a parent attempting to influence significant decisions of a child, as a group member attempting to influence the direction of the group, etc. The behaviors you employ as a leader have been learned over time, and are consistent enough that others come to expect you to act in certain predictable ways whenever functioning as a leader. Because leadership styles are learned they can be altered or replaced by new styles.

---

[1]Paul Hersey and Kenneth Blanchard, *Management of Organizational Behavior*, p. 84.

Behavior Themes and Bits
in Each Style

An effective leader must "play" many "parts"; sometimes holding the group together, sometimes challenging the group, while at other times standing "outside" of the group to act as a resource or expert. As a group, its situation changes, the leader's behavior (leadership style) must also change to remain fully effective and appropriate. As a leader moves from group to group, from situation to situation his/her leadership style should change to adapt to each new situation.

This concept of adaptive leadership may be summarized as follows:

Leadership is comprised of:

a cluster of *conceptual bits*:
the leader's "view" of persons, "view" of organization structures, his/her own education, role models, family relationships, theology, etc.

and

a cluster of *behavior bits*:
distinct acts of behavior; gestures, facial expressions, verbalization, words, etc.

which combine to make up *a behavior style*:
patterns of behavior used repeatedly in similar social situations.

several styles of acting combine into

a leadership role:
parts acted out in a social situation. The role is the part you are expected to "play."

There are several leadership roles a person can play:

in a *scene*:
social events in which interaction occurs; a business meeting, a party, at work, at home.[2]

A leader acts out his/her leadership role in a scene. For example, the leader is the chairper-

son in a meeting of the organization's finance committee. In that "role" he/she can use a variety of styles of leadership. He/she may be concerned with the poor relationships among several of the members of the group, or may "ride herd" on the group to get them to meet their goal in a recent fund drive, or may choose to be a "neutral" referee in the discussions of the group. Whatever style of leadership is chosen ought to be appropriate to the group and its situation. That style consists of specific behaviors, gestures, expressions, words that, taken together, accomplish the desired effect.

For example, if the leader is concerned with relationships in the group, he/she will say and do things that will give the group a sense of support and concern. This leader will behave in a relaxed manner, may tell a few jokes, show concern for the comfort of group members. He/she will probably provide refreshments, and will certainly compliment and praise the people for their work.

For a leader to be fully effective, he/she must know how to use a variety of leadership behaviors, as well as the needs of the group, and be able to use the leadership behaviors which will most appropriately meet those needs. This may mean selecting certain behaviors from his/her "bag" of leadership behaviors already learned, or it may require learning new behaviors.

Each of the leadership styles may be utilized with intentionality and a conscious decision to use it in a specific situation. Most leaders, however, have given little or no thought to the styles they use, rather they adopt a leadership style with little intentionality and are almost totally unconscious of the behavioral and conceptual bits which they use in that style.

As you proceed to work your way through this manual you will discover that, with the exception of the Slave and Martyr, which are always more-or-less inappropriate, **each of the styles and the bits of behavior which comprise it are appropriate in certain leadership situations. However, even appropriate styles can be acted out inappropriately.** This is generally the case when the leader acts out of blind conditioning having given no time to think through the differences between using a style in an ap-

---

[2]For a creative description of leadership styles and how they are comprised see Jerry Robinson and Roy Clifford, *Leadership Roles in Community Groups*, pp.

propriate, or in an inappropriate way.

In the following pages various leadership styles are described as well as some of the smaller behavior bits that accompany each style. These descriptions generalize. No one description "fits" anyone perfectly. These "portraits" are meant to identify groups of behaviors so that you may learn to be more intentional about your leadership behavior; choosing to keep certain styles of behavior, learning some new ones, adapting or discarding others.

Behavioral Versus Attitudinal Approaches To Understanding Leadership Style

Assessing one's leadership effectiveness from an attitudinal perspective (what I *THINK* about my leadership) and a behavioral perspective (what I actually *DO* in concrete situations) may present different pictures of one's leadership style.

Chris Argyris suggests we each have an "espoused theory" of our leadership style, and a "theory-in-use." [3] One's espoused theory is the way one wants to and/or believes he/she acts, while one's theory-in-use is the way he/she

actually does act in real life situations.

The materials in this manual are intended to help you look at your leadership style from a behavioral point of view. It is designed to help you reflect upon what you *do*, and how effective you are rather than merely what you *think* about leadership. [4]

DESCRIPTIONS OF LEADERSHIP STYLES

As you study the following material keep in mind that **each style can be used more-or-less appropriately or inappropriately. The descriptions will, therefore, list some behavior bits which are obviously appropriate and others which are more obviously inappropriate.** Exceptions to this are the behavior bits of the Slave and Martyr which are always more-or-less inappropriate leadership styles.

The terms used to identify each style are to be understood as illustrative only, and are not definitive. Actually, it would do no harm to the manual or the survey if no such terms were used at all and the reader relied entirely upon the definitions for understanding the styles.

---

[3] Chris Argyris and Donald Schon, THEORY IN PRACTICE. Jossey-Bass. 1974.

[4] This is where the "feedback forms" in the Leadership Kit, *How To Be A More Effective Church Leader*, become vital to your learning, since they allow you to look at your own leadership behavior (not attitude) through the eyes of others.

Passive Involvement:

The intent of this style is to cause a creative leadership vacuum in which group members can accomplish the task by assuming leadership roles and carrying on the work themselves. In order to do this the leader will become more-or-less passive and in some cases may withdraw from certain group meetings and activities altogether.

The use of this style requires the leader to be non-directive in group task oriented activities and to assume little or no responsibility for maintaining interpersonal relationships, thus making the group members responsible for task accomplishment and for monitoring their own relationships.

Other terms which have been used to describe leadership behavior similar to that which is described here are laissez-faire, abdicating, retiring.

The message communicated by this leader's behavior is "I know you can do that without me."

As a leadership style, passive involvement can be exhibited in varying degrees from a situation in which the leader is physically present but restrains from monitoring relationships and giving directions, to one in which the leader withdraws completely from the work setting.

In the first instance, the leader will participate in discussions and activities without taking positions in decision-making or setting directions and will allow the group to monitor its own relationships. In the second situation the leader will be absent altogether.

Behavior Themes	Behavior Bits
Withdraws	• Present with group but not involved in group's work. • Avoids meetings. "you'll do fine without me." • Avoids eye contact with group wanting help.
Postpones Action	• "Let's not do that now." • "I'm going to wait until someone takes action." • "I'm not the one responsible for that."
Avoids Responsibility	• Refuses assignments that can be given to others. • Will not pick up responsibilities others drop. • "I don't have time, why don't you do it?"

PersonOriented

Person Oriented:

The intent of this style is to actively monitor interpersonal relationships, thus creating a work climate in which group members will enjoy working together to accomplish the task. In order to do this the leader will, if necessary, concede his/her goals, and the organization's, in order to maintain conflict-free relationships.

The use of this style requires the leader to be flexible, quite permissive, person-oriented, and to take an active role in providing socio-emotional support. However, the leader places little emphasis on maintaining organizational structure and gives few directives.

Other terms which have been used to describe leadership behavior similar to the Person Oriented style are country club, cavalier, human relations.

The message communicated by this leader's behavior is, "I think you can do that on your own, but if not, I'll be here to advise you."

Some leaders adopt this style out of a healthy respect for the group's capabilities to do good work without much direction from him/herself. Other leaders using this style, however, have a more negative view of the group's capabilities. These leaders tend to view individuals in the group as fragile and unable to tolerate conflict or uncertainty. They feel, therefore, that the leader must ensure such situations do not develop, and if they do, to move quickly to correct them.

Behavior Themes	Behavior Bits
Entertains	• Enjoys a good joke. • Creates relaxed setting. • Playfulness welcome. • Encourages parties and celebrations.
Avoids Judgment	• Encourages one who fails; "Don't worry, Here, no one fails or succeeds alone, we are all in it together." • Creates a sense of equality and collegiality.
Gives Approval	• "You did a great job, thanks!" • "I like your idea." • "Feel free to do what you see needs doing. You don't need my approval."

Total Involvement

Gail Brogan

Total Involvement:

The intent of this style is to get everyone, the leader and all group members, fully involved in all phases of the group's planning and programming activities, while at the same time providing the necessary supervision to fully safeguard the interests of the organization. In order to do this the leader puts equal emphasis on maintaining human relationships, organizational structure, and on task-oriented effectiveness and/or efficiency.

This style requires the leader to be active and flexible in maintaining interpersonal relationships while at the same time providing necessary structure and supervision to ensure task accomplishment.

Other terms which have been used to describe leadership behavior similar to that which is described here are participative, activating, democratic.

The message communicated by this leader's behavior is, "We all have something to add in deciding what we're going to do and how we'll do it."

This leader clearly communicates his/her expectation that every person will be fully involved in seeing to it that the job is done, and done well. In order to ensure effective task ac-

complishment the leader will provide each individual, and the group, socio-emotional support, and will provide structures in which the group can participate in decision-making, problem-solving, and evaluation.

Behavior Themes	Behavior Bits
Initiates	• Encouraging attitude. • Solicits new ideas.
Involves	• Creates open atmosphere. • Repeats questions, listens actively. • Seeks support of others.
Assimilates	• "Is this what you mean?" • Structures and clarifies ideas. • "In summary, here is what we've agreed ...."
Reinforces	• "You did that well." • Gives credit, personalizes.
Solidifies	• "Let's review those points again." • Confirms agreements and decisions. • Summarizes.

Task Oriented

Task Oriented:

The intent of this style is to provide organizational structure and close supervision to ensure effective programs and/or efficient production of products and services.

Use of this style requires the leader to put major emphasis on the organization's programs and/or its products. This emphasis requires the leader be somewhat rigid and directive. Though not necessarily insensitive or uncaring toward persons, the task oriented leader views persons as secondary to the task. The value of individuals to the organization is judged in terms of what they can offer to it and do for it.

If necessary, the task oriented leader will risk damaging personal relationships in order to safeguard organizational interests and to ensure effective task accomplishment, and will not hesitate to use power and authority to ensure persons carry out his/her directives.

Other terms which have been used to describe leadership behavior similar to this are autocratic, benevolent dictator, controlling.

The message communicated by this leader's behavior is, "I will show you what to do and how to do it."

The Task Oriented leader will tend to relate to persons one-to-one, rather than in the group setting. This leader will also tend to control communication so that it flows from him/herself throughout the organization.

Behavior Themes	Behavior Bits
Regiments	• Appoints persons to their task, gives clear assignments. • Sets the agenda for business meetings.
Evaluates & Passes Judgment	• "You can do better than that." • "Follow my methods." • "This needs much improvement.
Establishes Dominance	• "I am God's person for this congregation." • "All new program ideas must be approved by me." • "I do not like the way you are handling our class, and ask for immediate changes."

The Martyr

Martyr:

The Martyr is one who places an extreme emphasis on the necessity of the leader's role in the organization, on task orientation, and on safeguarding the organization's structure. The Martyr attempts to maintain control by producing feelings of guilt and/or pity. The psychological forces which combine to make one a Martyr leader are:

1. A strong need to control.

2. A need to be revered.

3. A need to overwork (thus producing guilt and pity).

4. A basic concept that the group can never do the job well enough.

As such, the Martyr does more of the work than is appropriate, thus denying the group opportunity to experience effectiveness and to develop a healthy self-image.

The message communicated by this leader's behavior is, "You can't do anything without me, and I'm already doing it all."

The Martyr is often given to an exaggerated opinion of his/her own value to the organization and of the quality of his/her decisions and work. Given this, it follows that the Martyr will attempt to control all decisions and to do the work, since no one else in the organization can make decisions or carry them out as well as he/she can.

Behavior Themes	Behavior Bits
Enforces Norms	• "The book says ...do it that way." • "As you sow, so shall you reap." • "You know what the rules say."
Overworks Self	• "Let me do it. I hope it won't kill me." • Runs around alot. Preoccupied with trivia. • No days off, no vacations. • First to office, last to leave.
Seeks Pity	• "I work so hard, but I never catch up." • "If only someone else around here would do something." • "You go ahead on home, I'll stay here and finish the work.

The Slave

Gail S Brogan

Slave:

The Slave is one who places an extreme emphasis on passive involvement. The Slave totally withdraws from leadership responsibility while doing more work than is appropriate.

The psychological forces which combine to make one a Slave leader are:

1. A strong need to feel needed.
2. A need to avoid any semblance of conflict, and to have pleasant interpersonal relationships.
3. A need to overwork.
4. A basic concept that the group can never do the job well enough.

As such, many of the same forces which cause some to be martyr leaders cause others to be slave leaders, except that the slave tries to assuage guilt rather than cause it. By doing more work than is appropriate, the slave leader denies the group opportunity to experience effectiveness and to develop a healthy self-image. The Slave avoids decision-making, overworks self, strives to please.

The message communicated by this leader's behavior is, "Don't worry about it, I'll get it done."

The slave is often given to a sense of worthlessness or guilt unless constantly occupied by some activity. He/she, however, often feels unable and/or unworthy to handle jobs of significant responsibility. The Slave, therefore, will often engage in "busy work" and will carry on a great flurry of activities in order to avoid decisions or problems and to avoid becoming involved in tasks of greater responsibility. And, of course, the Slave will always want all the others to see just how busy he/she is.

Behavior Themes	Behavior Bits
Assuages	• "Don't worry about it, I"ll do it for you." • "That's OK ... no one will know."
Overworks Self	• Preoccupied with busy work. • Desk always cluttered. • No days off, few vacations.
Avoids Decisions	• Misses crucial meetings and phone calls. • Busy with a flurry of activities to avoid taking important responsibilities.
Strives to Please	• Needs to be needed. • Poor self-image, sense of worthlessness.

The Lord, Jesus, was the most effective leader who ever lived. Following is a simple test for you to apply your learnings regarding the leadership styles by reviewing various situations in which Christ, himself, utilized the four appropriate leadership styles.

On the chart below, please provide the missing information:

Situation	Scripture Reference	Leadership Style Christ Used	Check One
1. The scribes and pharisees bring an adulteress to him for judgment.	John 8:3-9	Passive Involvement Person Oriented Total Involvement Task Oriented	☐ ☐ ☐ ☐

What did Christ do here that prompted your selection?

2. With the woman after the scribes and pharisees leave	John 8:10-11	Passive Involvement Person Oriented Total Involvement Task Oriented	☐ ☐ ☐ ☐

What did Christ do here that prompted your selection?

3. Feeding the five thousand	Matt. 14:15-21	Passive Involvement Person Oriented Total Involvement Task Oriented	☐ ☐ ☐ ☐

What did Christ do here that prompted your selection?

4. Cleansing the temple	Matt. 21:12-13	Passive Involvement Person Oriented Total Involvement Task Oriented	☐ ☐ ☐ ☐

What did Christ do here that prompted your selection?

ANSWERS: No. 1, Passive Involvement; No. 2, Person Oriented; No. 3, Total Involvement; No. 4, Task Oriented.

CONCERNS THAT DETERMINE LEADERSHIP STYLES and THE LEADERSHIP STYLES MATRIX

Are leaders born or made? Do leaders emerge as a response to a situation? Is there a list of traits that is common to all leaders? Many theories have been put forth about leadership. Long ago Ceaser Lombroso, an Italian anthropologist, held that leadership style could be determined by the shape of a person's skull or the bumps on his head. Other theorists held that body types determined one's leadership style.[1]

More recent studies support a dynamic view of leadership namely, that leadership is a function of the leader, the followers, and the situation (L = f(l,f,s)). Leadership is effective when a leader correctly assesses the needs of the group, understands the situation of the group, and chooses a leadership style and behaviors that are appropriate.

---

[1]Jerry Robinson and Roy Clifford, *Leadership Roles in Community Groups*, p. 3.

Since the late 1940's, public and private institutions and American universities have cooperated in extensive research into leadership and its effects upon the persons and organizations which are being led. All major leadership studies have indicated there are two fundamental concerns felt by every leader:

1. A concern for the PEOPLE who are being led.

2. A concern that the TASK be accomplished satisfactorily.

Effective leadership requires the ability to make intentional choices regarding the amount of emphasis the leader will give to caring for the people in the organization, as well as the amount of emphasis given to insuring the task is accomplished satisfactorily.

Ohio State Leadership Studies[2]

Ohio State University was the first to conduct major studies into leadership. The studies identified the two basic leadership concerns, referring to them as:

1. Consideration: leader behavior to promote friendship, mutual trust, respect, and warmth in the relationships between the leader and the people.

2. Initiating Structure: leader behavior to establish channels of communication, organizational policies, and procedurial methods; all intended to define the working relationships between leader and people, and the manner in which the work assignments are carried out.

The Michigan Studies[3]

Following the Ohio State Studies, the Survey Research Center at the University of Michigan did a study which identified two basic leadership concerns, labeling them as:

1. Employee-centered behavior.

2. Production-centered behavior.

Summarizing the results of this Michigan study, Vroom says, "There is in this work substantial evidence indicating that more effective leaders (1) tend to have relationships with their subordinates which are supportive and enhance the latter's sense of personal worth and importance, (2) use group rather than man-

to-man methods of supervision and decision-making, and (3) tend to set high performance goals."[4]

The Blake-Mouton Managerial Grid[5]

The studies, above, paved the way for the understanding that a leader's behavior is comprised of a mix of the two leadership concerns and each concern can be emphasized to a greater or lesser degree thus resulting in a variety of behavioral leadership styles.

Building upon the Ohio State and Michigan Studies, in 1965 Blake and Mouton developed the "Managerial Grid" to illustrate the various leadership styles which may result from differing degrees of emphasis being given to the two basic leader concerns. They did this by first diagramming two axes to illustrate a low and a high degree of emphasis for each concern, as follows:[6]

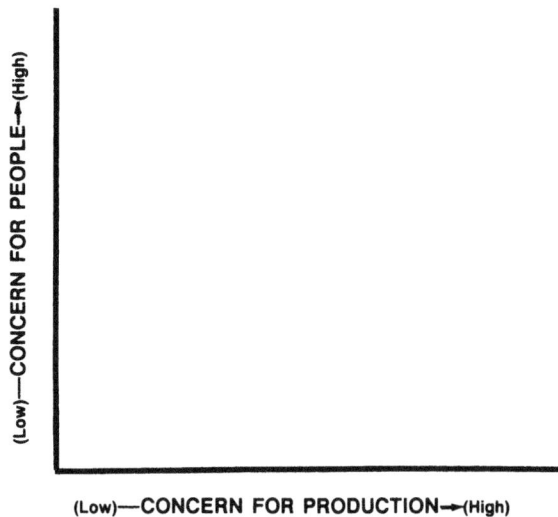

(Low)—CONCERN FOR PRODUCTION→(High)

Figure 4.1

With this as a starting point, they went on to create a grid illustrating the various possible combinations of the basic concerns. Finally, they gave stylistically descriptive names to each of the combinations, and added a scale

[2] "Leadership," Victor Vroom, in *Handbook of Industrial and Organizational Psychology*, Marvin Dunnette, ed., Rand McNally, 1976, pp. 1530-31.

[3] Vroom, pp. 1531-33.

[4] Vroom, p. 1532.

[5] *The Managerial Grid III*, Robert Blake and Jane Mouton, Gulf Publishing Co., 1985. This book should be on your list for "must reading."

[6] Blake and Mouton, p. 12.

to measure the degree of emphasis given to each concern within each style combination. The result was the Managerial Grid, below:[7]

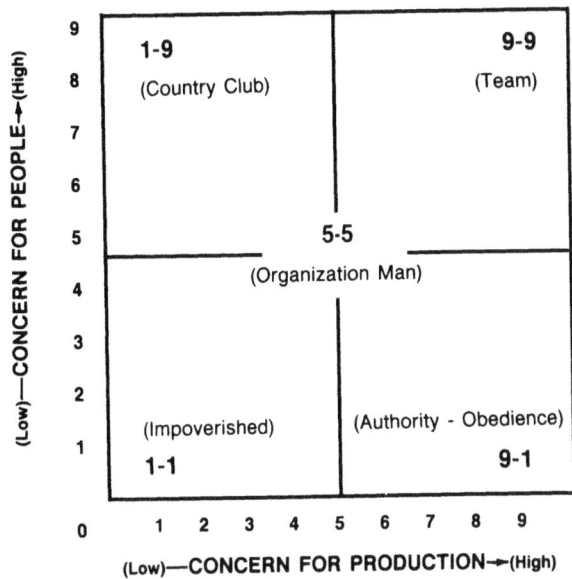

Figure 4.2

In defining the grid, the authors state, "Concern for production and concern for people . . . can be . . . pictured as continuum from a minimum amount (1) to a maximum amount (9), with intermediate degrees of concern in between."[7] Therefore the leadership style characterized by the 1-1 quadrant would place low emphasis on both concern for people and concern for production, while the leadership style depicted in the 9-1 quadrant would place high emphasis on concern for production and low emphasis on concern for people. The 1-9 quadrant characterizes a leadership style which places low emphasis on production concern and high emphasis on people concern, while the 9-9 quadrant places high emphasis on both production and people concerns. The 5-5 style is a compromise of all the others.

The "Managerial Grid" has become an immensely popular theoretical model contributing to much of the best current literature on leadership and organizational behavior.[8],

In the matrix, the Slave style is set in the Passive Involvement quadrant to illustrate it as a variation of that style. The leader adopting the Passive Involvement style leaves the group alone to do the work, while the Slave does the work for them. Likewise, the Martyr style is a variation of the Task Oriented style. The Martyr attempts to gain control by use of guilt and/or pity. For the situations included in the survey, the Slave and Martry styles are never appropriate leadership behaviors.

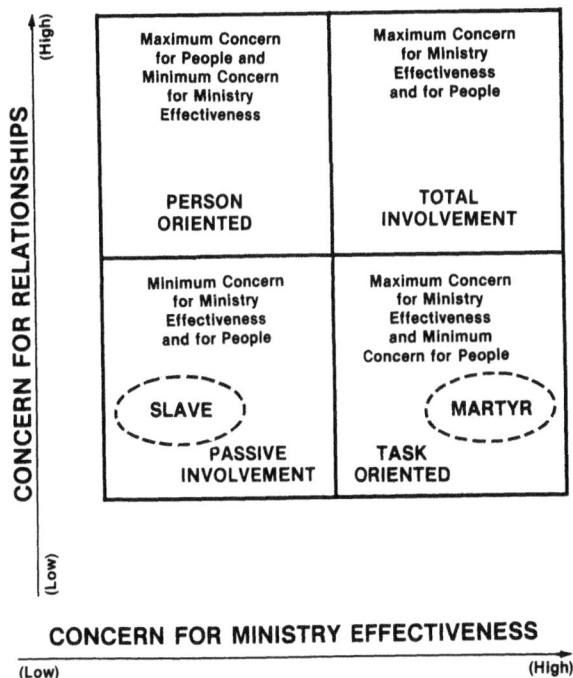

CONCERN FOR MINISTRY EFFECTIVENESS
(Low)   (High)

Figure 4.3

The Matrix Used in this Study

For the purposes of our study two additional leadership styles will be introduced: the Slave and the Martyr; and the two basic leadership concerns will be referred to as: **Concern for Relationships** and **Concern for Organizational Structure/Task Effectiveness** (more simply, **Concern for Ministry Effectiveness**). Figure 4.3 illustrates the matrix and locates the leadership styles.

[7] Blake and Mouton, p. 208.

[8] One such book which should be on your list for "must reading" is, *Management of Organizational Behavior*, Hersey and Blanchard, Prentice-Hall, 1977.

Both the Slave and Martyr leaders always do more work than is appropriate. The group may come to expect and depend upon this, thus regressing to a permanent state of passive dependency upon the leader.

The leader's degree of commitment to each of the two basic leadership concerns, Relationships and Task Effectiveness, determines his/her leadership style. For example, a person who is highly task oriented but has low concern for maintaining interpersonal relationships is experienced by others as a controlling or directive leader; while the leader having high concern for relationships but low concern for programs or products is experienced as a relational or person-oriented leader. The leader having low concern for both, relationships and task-ministry orientation, is experienced as a passive or laissez faire leader; and the leader having a high concern for both is experienced as an activating or participative leader.

The Tannenbaum & Schmidt Continuum of Leader Behavior

Robert Tannenbaum and Warren Schmidt developed another helpful model for conceptualizing leadership behavior as running along a continuum from an authoritarian style, where task accomplishment is the leader's most basic concern, to a democratic style, where the leader gives much more task responsibility to the group while giving his/her attention to maintaining the interpersonal relationships, below:[9]

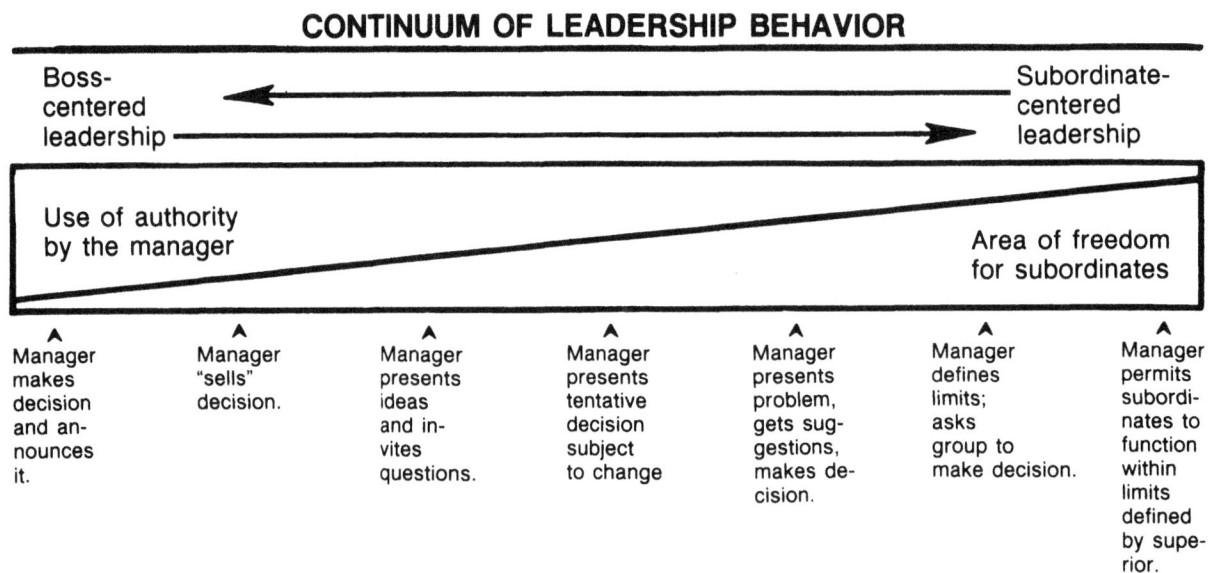

CONTINUUM OF LEADERSHIP BEHAVIOR

Boss-centered leadership						Subordinate-centered leadership

Use of authority by the manager

Area of freedom for subordinates

Manager makes decision and announces it.	Manager "sells" decision.	Manager presents ideas and invites questions.	Manager presents tentative decision subject to change	Manager presents problem, gets suggestions, makes decision.	Manager defines limits; asks group to make decision.	Manager permits subordinates to function within limits defined by superior.

[9] "How to Choose a Leadership Pattern," *Harvard Business Review*, Robert Tannenbaum and Warren H. Schmidt, March-April 1957, pp. 95-101.

TOOLS FOR DETERMINING
A GROUP'S LEADERSHIP NEEDS
and
SELECTING THE MOST
EFFECTIVE LEADERSHIP STYLE

In order to be fully effective a leader must develop two important skills; the ability to employ a variety of leadership behaviors and the ability to determine which set of behaviors would be most effective with a particular group at a given point in time. Stated another way, a leader must be able to match the most appropriate leadership style to the group's level of ability to perform a given task.

STEP 5: Develop skills in determining the leadership needs of a group

Some leaders are capable of using a wide variety of leadership styles; others are more limited. The survey in Step 2 of this manual helped you identify your leadership styles. Step 3 described some of the behaviors that contribute to each style. This is important learning for you as you work to become a more effective group leader.

A second requirement for effective leadership is the ability to determine what a group (or person) actually needs by way of leadership; that is, what style of leadership will most likely enable the group to be most effective and motivated to accomplish its ministry task.

This is an entirely new concept for most leaders who tend to use the same leadership style with every group, regardless of differences between one group and another. All groups are not the same, however, and an effective leader must be able to meet each group "where it is" in terms of its own ability to carry out its ministry assignment.

GROUP MATURITY

A leader, then, must not only know what leadership behaviors he/she possesses. He/she must also be able to "read" the maturity level of the group. The concept of group maturity refers to a group's willingness and ability to take responsibility for planning and carrying out its work.

In his book, *Making Meetings Work*, Leland Bradford has an excellent chapter dealing with the "characteristics of a mature group."[1] In it he says, "to achieve maximum efficiancy and high member satisfaction, (groups) need to strive for maturity through deliberate, systematic efforts. Groups do not grow haphazardly, nor is maturity automatic . . . . Many groups, unfortunately, remain at an immature level because little effort is made to keep the group in good working order."[2] Bradford introduces the idea that it is possible to view groups as being at various stages of maturity, much as one might view the various stages of maturity in a person. Perhaps the following chart may serve to illustrate this fact.

STAGES OF DEVELOPMENT

	Immature	No Longer Totally Immature But Not Yet Fully Mature		Mature
Individual	Infant	Childhood	Adolescense	Adult
Group	Unable and/or unwilling to carry out its responsibilities	Somewhat able and willing	More able and willing	Fully capable and willing to carry out its responsibilities

Figure 5.1

Even as there are two basic concerns which combine to determine the leader's style, so there are two basic conditions which combine to determine a group's level of maturity relative to its work responsibilities: They are:

1. The quality of interpersonal relationships among group members, and with the leader.

2. The amount of skill and ability the group has which qualifies it to plan and carry out a specific task, and its commitment to apply these abilities to the task.

These two basic group conditions combine to determine a group's maturity or immaturity, and it is the group's degree of maturity or immaturity which determines the appropriateness and effectiveness of one's leadership behavior. We can now expand our diagram to illustrate the relationship between the most appropriate leadership style and a group's level of maturity:

[1] *Making Meetings Work: A Guide for Leaders and Group Members*, Leland B. Bradford, University Associates, 1976. A book for your "must" reading.
[2] Bradford, p. 29.

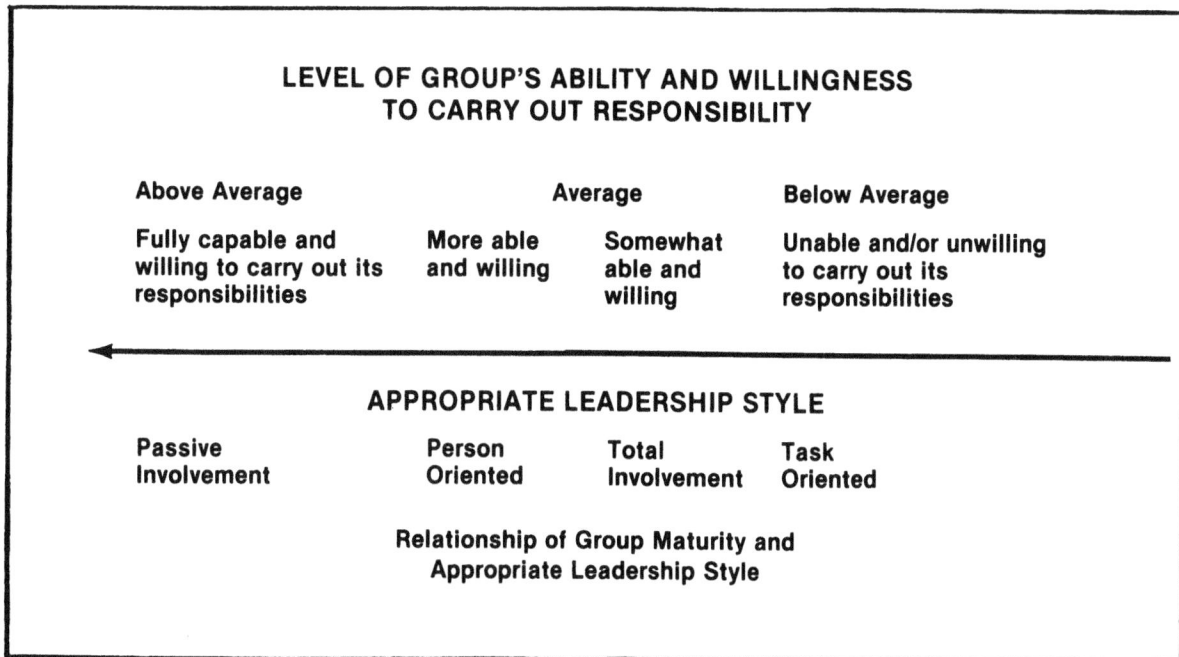

**LEVEL OF GROUP'S ABILITY AND WILLINGNESS
TO CARRY OUT RESPONSIBILITY**

Above Average   **Average**   **Below Average**

**Fully capable and   More able   Somewhat   Unable and/or unwilling
willing to carry out its and willing able and   to carry out its
responsibilities   willing   responsibilities**

◄───

APPROPRIATE LEADERSHIP STYLE

**Passive   Person   Total   Task
Involvement   Oriented   Involvement   Oriented**

**Relationship of Group Maturity and
Appropriate Leadership Style**

Figure 5.2

The diagram, above, illustrates that as a group's maturity level increases leadership behavior, to remain appropriate, requires less and less structure (task) accompanied by increased socio-emotional support (relationships). Then, as the group eventually moves toward above average maturity, the leader responds by decreasing socio-emotional support.

This reality carries tremendous implications regarding a leader's effectiveness as he/she moves from one group to another, or as a group, itself, moves from one task situation to another. For example, a school principal, in order to remain fully effective in every situation, would likely have to vary his/her leadership behavior when dealing with the kindergarten class from that used when dealing with the school board, or the faculty. Varying levels of group maturity and development call for different leadership styles and behaviors.

GROWING TOWARD MATURITY

Groups, like individuals, can be motivated and equipped to grow toward maturity. The leader's ability to continually monitor the group's progress (or regress) and to match it with the appropriate leadership behavior is a key factor in determining whether the group will tend toward greater levels of maturity.

Increasing group maturity requires that the group is growing along a number of dimensions; some dealing with the group's task specific abilities, and others dealing with the group's interpersonal relationships.[3]

A listing of characteristics for analyzing a group's immaturity — maturity, and how they are experienced in groups are listed on the following pp. 36-38.

---

[3] Several taxonomies have been developed to identify the dimensions to look for in assessing a group's maturity level; i.e., Leland Bradford, *Making Meetings Work*, pp. 29-34, and Chris Argyris in *Management of Organizational Behavior*, pp. 62 & 309.

CHARACTERISTICS OF A MATURE GROUP

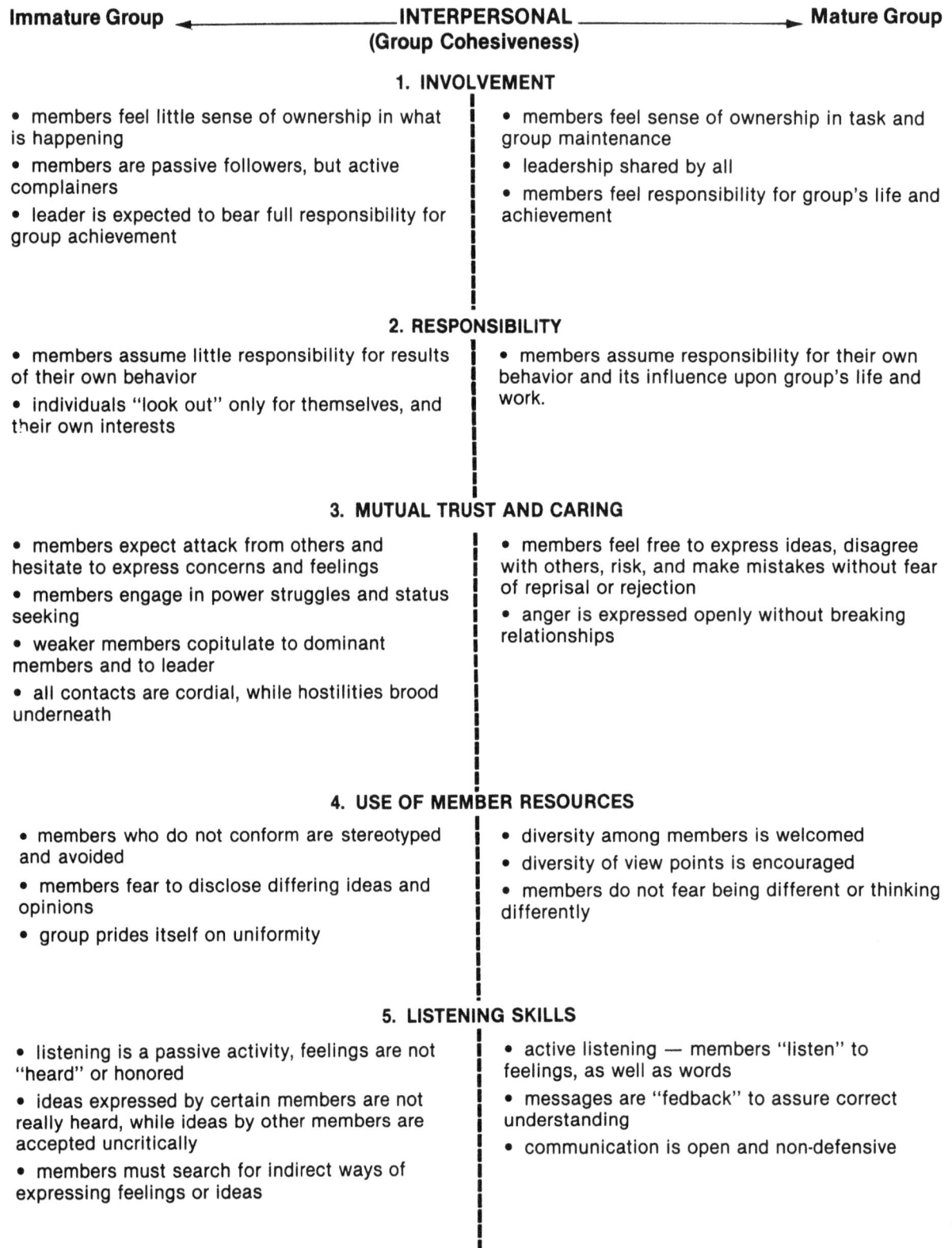

Immature Group ◄——————————— INTERPERSONAL ——————————► Mature Group
(Group Cohesiveness)

1. INVOLVEMENT

• members feel little sense of ownership in what is happening	• members feel sense of ownership in task and group maintenance
• members are passive followers, but active complainers	• leadership shared by all
• leader is expected to bear full responsibility for group achievement	• members feel responsibility for group's life and achievement

2. RESPONSIBILITY

• members assume little responsibility for results of their own behavior	• members assume responsibility for their own behavior and its influence upon group's life and work.
• individuals "look out" only for themselves, and their own interests	

3. MUTUAL TRUST AND CARING

• members expect attack from others and hesitate to express concerns and feelings	• members feel free to express ideas, disagree with others, risk, and make mistakes without fear of reprisal or rejection
• members engage in power struggles and status seeking	• anger is expressed openly without breaking relationships
• weaker members copitulate to dominant members and to leader	
• all contacts are cordial, while hostilities brood underneath	

4. USE OF MEMBER RESOURCES

• members who do not conform are stereotyped and avoided	• diversity among members is welcomed
• members fear to disclose differing ideas and opinions	• diversity of view points is encouraged
• group prides itself on uniformity	• members do not fear being different or thinking differently

5. LISTENING SKILLS

• listening is a passive activity, feelings are not "heard" or honored	• active listening — members "listen" to feelings, as well as words
• ideas expressed by certain members are not really heard, while ideas by other members are accepted uncritically	• messages are "fedback" to assure correct understanding
• members must search for indirect ways of expressing feelings or ideas	• communication is open and non-defensive

6. ACCEPTING NEW MEMBERS

- group pressures new members to conform
- ideas and resources of new members are not recognized, or are rejected
- new members must fight their way into the group
- new members are overtly welcomed, but covertly are not trusted, or are resented

- group is sensitive to new member's need to be included
- group views new member as potential resource
- new members are accepted on their own terms and not pressured to conform
- group recognizes accepting new members call for change on its own part

7. HIDDEN AGENDAS

- group fails to recognize hidden agendas exist, and lacks the skill to bring them to the surface
- group fears dealing with such matters, and punishes those who confess holding such ideas

- group recognizes persons hesitant to disclose concerns which are self-oriented, and encourages such matters be discused openly

Immature Group ◄─────────── GROUP SKILL & ABILITY ──────────► Mature Group

1. GOAL SETTING & PLANNING

- group has no clear sense of its mission
- group is unable to set meaningful goals and plans for achieving them, spends much of its time "putting out fires"
- group settles for less than its best effort

- group has clear sense of its mission and its hoped-for results
- group is able to set meaningful targets and realistic plans for achieving them
- group approaches its work with intentionality, motivation and commitment

2. EXPERIMENTATION

- group adheres to rigid behavior
- group is fearful of risk, and mistakes are critized and/or punished
- a "we've always done it this way," or "come weal or woe our status is quo" attitude prevails

- group experiments with new resources and work methods
- new, untested ideas are welcomed to expand thinking and strategies
- group is willing to risk and mistakes are not punished but used as opportunities for further learning

3. EVALUATION

- group seldom deals with internal problems until they become debilitating, then a "scapegoat" is dealt with in a punishing and destructive manner
- group avoids program evaluation because of a fear of the results

- group examines its own operation without defensiveness, and willingly diverts attention from the task to correct group life problems
- group seeks evaluation feedback regarding results of its work
- group possesses ability to use evaluation not only to correct present problems, but also to strengthen future programs

4. USING SUBGROUPS

- distrusts the work or decisions of subgroups thus accepting only the work of the entire group
- label subgroups as "cliques" and dangerous to group interests

- accepts and makes use of various subgroups based upon mutuality of style, interests, and interpersonal likings
- trusts important assignments and decisions on behalf of total group
- makes resources available to encourage subgroup's unique interests and work

5. FLIGHT BEHAVIOR

- fails to recognize differences between needed rest and flight
- leaders "push harder" as group grows less productive and more weary
- views times of rest and play as a waste of money and time

- recognizes differences between flight, avoidance from the task due to fear, lack of interest from the need for relaxation and "just being together"
- sensitive to the need for change in tempo
- plans group opportunity for informal socializing and play

6. DEALING WITH CONFLICT

- views conflict as dangerous and to be avoided at all costs
- denies presence of conflict, "sweeps it under the rug" as long as possible
- when conflict finally erupts, everyone seeks to win by whatever means necessary; those who are afraid to fight withdraw altogether

- recognizes conflict can strengthen group ties and help clarify goals and procedures
- possesses skills to manage conflict constructively
- faces conflict squarely and openly
- sees conflict as a problem to be solved rather than a battle to be won

7. DECISION-MAKING

- decisions are made by leader and/or a few dominate members; others are passive
- blames leader and dominate members for any failure
- each one insists on "having things their own way," thus stalling many important decisions indefinitely

- works together with leader to make decisions
- assumes responsibility for results
- commits resources necessary to ensure decisions become reality

DETERMINING A GROUP'S LEVEL OF MATURITY

We have used the group characteristics to develop the following two worksheets to help you determine the task relevant maturity level of a group.

Worksheet No. 1 is designed to help determine a group's general level of maturity as it relates to all the tasks or responsibilities of the group.

Worksheet No. 2 is designed to help determine a group's level of maturity as it relates to a specific task or responsibility.

In determining a group's maturity level no moral judgment is implied. You are not assessing the worth of persons, you are evaluating their effectiveness as a group on a relative scale of performance. The purpose of these worksheets, then, is not to judge persons but to help you choose the leadership style and behaviors most appropriate to the group.

You may use the worksheets alone. Whenever possible, however, it is advisable to involve several members (or all) of the group in the process.

COMPONENTS OF GROUP MATURITY

The first seven items on the two worksheets describe a group's cohesiveness—ways group members relate to each other and/or to the leader. You might ask, "What is the *nature* and *quality* of interpersonal relationships among group members, with the leader, and with others outside the group?"

The last seven items on the group maturity worksheet describe the amount of skill and ability the group has to plan and implement its tasks. You might ask, "How does this group address and perform its tasks?"

It is important to note that while group maturity can be seen from these two perspectives, there is a close relationship between them. Highly cohesive groups are more effective in goal achievement than low cohesive groups. Task concerns may also influence relationships. For example, clarity about goals and effectiveness tend to foster group cohesiveness. Therefore, when you think of the group maturity continuum, consider all the components as being interrelated and affecting the whole construct of group maturity. That is, when you make changes in one component, that change will influence all other components.

USING WORKSHEET NO. 1

1. Circle the number on each continuum on the GROUP ASSESSMENT WORKSHEET which you feel best represents the group's position relative to that item.

2. Connect all of the circled numbers with a line, creating a profile of the group.

3. If group members are also using the worksheet, first complete your own assessment, steps 1 and 2, above, then have the group members do likewise.

4. Prepare a profile of the group members' responses by locating the area on each continuum where the group members' responses tend to cluster or, if you wish, find the mean ($\bar{x}$) average of their responses on each continuum. Prepare a worksheet showing the "clustering" or the "average" group response for each continuum.

5. Study your own worksheet profile, and the group's, if it was involved, to determine the level of group maturity most descriptive of the group.

How To Assess Your Group's Readiness and Ability to Work Effectively:
A Group Assessment Worksheet—No. 1

Your Name: _____ Date: _____

Group: _____

Following are fourteen items that describe the way in which group members relate to one another, and how they go about their work. Each item is presented on a scale of 1-8. At either end of the scale is a description of that item which is quite opposite in meaning from the description at the other end of the scale. The numbers along the scales indicate a variety of responses, one of which you are requested to circle for each item. An example is given below:

Concern only
for Oneself   **Concern for**
                                                                                                        Each Other

1	2	3	4	5	6	7	8
Agree very strongly	Agree strongly	Agree somewhat	Agree slightly	Agree slightly	Agree somewhat	Agree strongly	Agree very strongly

If you would "agree somewhat" that members of your group demonstrate a concern for others you would circle #6. However, should you "agree strongly" that the members of the group demonstrate a concern only for themselves, you would circle #2.

1. Circle the number for each item you feel best describes your group's position relative to that item. Circle only one number for each item.
2. Connect the circled numbers with a line.
3. Study the worksheet to determine your overall impression of your group.

In these seven items think of ways group members relate to each other and/or to the leader.

Passive..(Involvement)..Active

| 1 | 2 | 3 | 4 | 5 | 6 | 7 | 8 |

This item assesses the ability of the group to dynamically interrelate with the leader and one another. To what extent does the group act on its own, or does it wait for the leader to tell it what to do and how to do it? Do the members actively participate in meetings, take positions, demonstrate enthusiasm in attending the meetings and in carrying out assignments?

Dependent Upon Leader......................(Responsibility)..........................Shoulders Responsibility

| 1 | 2 | 3 | 4 | 5 | 6 | 7 | 8 |

This item assesses the ability of the group to assume responsibility for planning and carrying out its work. To what extent can the group carry out its responsibilities in the absence of the leader? Can the leader delegate task responsibilities and expect the group to carry them out in a satisfactory manner?

Distrust and Non-Caring.................(Mutual Trust and Caring).....................Caring For One Another

| 1 | 2 | 3 | 4 | 5 | 6 | 7 | 8 |

This item assesses the extent to which group members are concerned for one another, and for others outside of the group. To what extent is the group self-serving, or does it see its mission as serving the world beyond? Do members focus attention and resources upon themselves, with a high regard for power and control over others?

Stresses
Member Conformity..........................(Use of Member Resources)................Member Diversity

Full Use Of

| 1 | 2 | 3 | 4 | 5 | 6 | 7 | 8 |

This item assesses the extent to which the group is concerned to discover and utilize the unique contributions of each member. To what extent are differing opinions and styles allowed? Are members stereotyped and "punished" for being different, or is diversity welcomed?

Passive Listening,
Closed Communications.....................(Listening Skills)..................Open Communications

Active Listening

| 1 | 2 | 3 | 4 | 5 | 6 | 7 | 8 |

This item assesses the ability of group members to clearly state their opinions, and to "listen" to others even when they disagree. To what extent are members able to express emotions as well as ideas? Does communication flow in all directions, or does it tend to flow to and from the leader? Are persons able to "read" non-verbal messages; body language, facial expressions?

Self-Effacing New
New Member Assimilation ....(Accepting New Members) ....**Self-Enhancing,**
Member Assimilation

| 1 | 2 | 3 | 4 | 5 | 6 | 7 | 8 |

This item assesses the ability to assimilate new members without creating sub-groups of "senior" and "junior" participants. To what extent is the group sensitive to new members' needs to be included? Are new members welcomed as persons of worth, with an important contribution, or must they prove themselves?

Personal Agendas
Kept Secret ....(Hidden Agendas) ....**Personal Agendas**
Freely Disclosed

| 1 | 2 | 3 | 4 | 5 | 6 | 7 | 8 |

This item assesses the ability of the group to "own" their positions and desires for the group. To what extent do members fear disclosing concerns which are self-oriented, or in opposition to prevailing group opinions? Is the group able to recognize when hidden agendas are present and interfering with group process?

In these seven items think of ways the group performs its tasks.

Goal Confusion
No Future Planning ....(Goal Setting and Planning) ....**Sets Clear Goals &**
Long Range Plans

| 1 | 2 | 3 | 4 | 5 | 6 | 7 | 8 |

This item assesses the group's willingness to be intentional about its work, and its ability to decide step-by-step approaches to doing what it wants to do. To what extent does the group clearly know what it wants to accomplish, and the steps necessary to accomplish it? Does the group strategize its work before it begins? Are members willing to accept specific assignments and carry them out?

Ridged Behavior ....(Experimentation) ....**Adaptive, Flexible**
Behavior

| 1 | 2 | 3 | 4 | 5 | 6 | 7 | 8 |

This item assesses the willingness of the group to modify its position or behavior to more appropriately respond to new conditions. To what extent does the group always work to maintain the status quo? Are persons willing to compromise in order to maintain working relationships with others? To adopt new ideas or behaviors?

No Evaluation ....(Evaluation) ....**Openly Evaluates Its**
Programs

| 1 | 2 | 3 | 4 | 5 | 6 | 7 | 8 |

This item assesses the ability and willingness of the group to reflect on its own actions, to measure the quality of its programs, and to allow this information to influence future programming. To what extent does the group candidly look at the results of its own behavior and programs? Are persons open to receiving, and able to give, critical feedback to other members?

**All Work Done
In Total Groups**..(Using Sub Groups)..**Delegates
Responsibility**

   1   2   3   4   5   6   7   8

This item assesses the extent to which the group trusts individuals in small groups to carry out important assignments on its behalf. To what extent is work delegated? If work is delegated, to what extent does the group trust small group discussions? Does it insist on reviewing and revising all work done by small groups?

**Fears innovation,
Avoids Any Risk**...(Flight Behavior)..**Welcomes Innovative
"Risk" Filled Challenges**

   1   2   3   4   5   6   7   8

This item assesses the group's ability to confront difficult or distasteful tasks. To what extent does the group recognize the difference between avoidance behavior and the need for relaxation, or "just being" together? To what extent is the group sensitive to the need for changes of tempo in work behavior?

Denies, Avoids Conflict...................................(Dealing With Conflict)..........................**Openly Recognizes Conflict**

   1   2   3   4   5   6   7   8

This item assesses the group's ability to constructively deal with conflict. To what extent does the group encourage differences of opinions or does it attempt to squelch differences? When conflict does arise, is it dealt with openly and without damage to relationships, or are members' feeling hurt, do persons withdraw, etc?

**Leaders Make
Decisions**..(Decision making)..**Participative
Decision-Making**

   1   2   3   4   5   6   7   8

This item assesses the ability of the group to work together with the leader to make decisions, and its willingness to assume responsibility for the results. To what extent are the members willing to work together in reaching decisions which will commit group resources? Do persons insist on "having things their own way"? Does the group defer to the leader in decision making?

Printed copies of this worksheet are available from the publisher.

How To Assess Your Group's Readiness and Ability to Carry Out a Specific Task:
A Group Assessment Worksheet—No. 2

Your Name: _____ Date: _____

Group: _____

Specific Task/Responsibility to be Performed: _____

_____

Following are ten items that pertain to the way in which the group members can be expected to relate to one another, and how they tend to go about their work when dealing with a task/responsibility similar to the one listed above.

Please **circle one number on each scale** of each item to rate the group's willingness and ability to do this particular task.

---

1. How much experience has the group had with tasks similar to this one?

8	7	6	5	4	3	2	1
A great deal			Some				None at all

List the tasks you have in mind:

1.

2.

3.

2. How effective was the group in handling the previous similar tasks?

8	7	6	5	4	3	2	1
Highly effective			About Average				Not at all

List specific situations and results:

1.

2.

3.

3. How effective has the group been in handling the last three non-similar tasks?

| 8 | 7 | 6 | 5 | 4 | 3 | 2 | 1 |

Highly effective   So-So   Very low effectiveness

List the three tasks you had in mind:

1.

2.

3.

4. Generally, how does the group go about planning and carrying out its work?

| 8 | 7 | 6 | 5 | 4 | 3 | 2 | 1 |

Will plan and carry   So-So   Waits for
out on its own   the leader

5. How effective is the group in identifying and solving unexpected problems?

| 8 | 7 | 6 | 5 | 4 | 3 | 2 | 1 |

Highly effective   So-So   Very ineffective

- -

6. Have group members demonstrated an interest in obtaining skills training to improve effectiveness?

| 8 | 7 | 6 | 5 | 4 | 3 | 2 | 1 |

Highly motivated   Some   Very reluctant to
to gain new skills   put forth necessary
on their own   time and effort

7. To what extent does the group already possess the necessary skills for this responsibility?

| 8 | 7 | 6 | 5 | 4 | 3 | 2 | 1 |

Has all   Has some of the   Has none of the
necessary skills   necessary skills   necessary skills

8. To what extent does the group "stick to the job" until it is satisfactorily completed?

| 8 | 7 | 6 | 5 | 4 | 3 | 2 | 1 |

Always   So-So   Very poor record

9. To what extent are group members trusting and supportive of one another?

| 8 | 7 | 6 | 5 | 4 | 3 | 2 | 1 |

High trust   So-So   Much competition
and support   and distrust

10. To what extent does the group welcome new challenges and increased responsibility?

| 8 | 7 | 6 | 5 | 4 | 3 | 2 | 1 |

Always seeking   So-So   Resists new
new challenges   challenges and
and responsibilities   responsibilities

Questions 1 - 5 deal with issues related to the group's ability to handle the task. Questions 6 -10 are related to interpersonal relationships among group members, and the group's willingness to improve skills and relationships. You may now score your group according to the responses you gave to the items dealing with each of the two issues.

1. Find the mean ($\bar{x}$) average of your responses to questions 1 - 5 (total your responses and divide by 5).
   _____ mean average score.

2. Find the mean ($\bar{x}$) average of your responses to questions 6 - 10 (total your responses and divide by 5).
   _____ mean average score.

If several members of the group completed worksheets you may find the average scores they gave to the group as follows:

1. Total all responses for questions 1 - 5 and divide by the number of persons who completed worksheets.
   _____ average group response.

2. Total all responses for questions 6 - 10 and divide by the number of persons who completed worksheets.
   _____ average group response.

The diagram below is provided for you to plot your scores:

1. On the left hand axis, **Task Effectiveness**, plot your average score for questions 1 - 5.

2. On the right hand axis, **Relationships**, plot your average score for questions 6 - 10.

These two scores indicate the degree of emphasis the group leader should give to each of these concerns in his/her own leadership behavior. The scores also say something about the issues the group should consider in its own efforts to improve its effectiveness.

For a single rough score, draw a straight line between the two scores, causing an intersection with the middle axis.

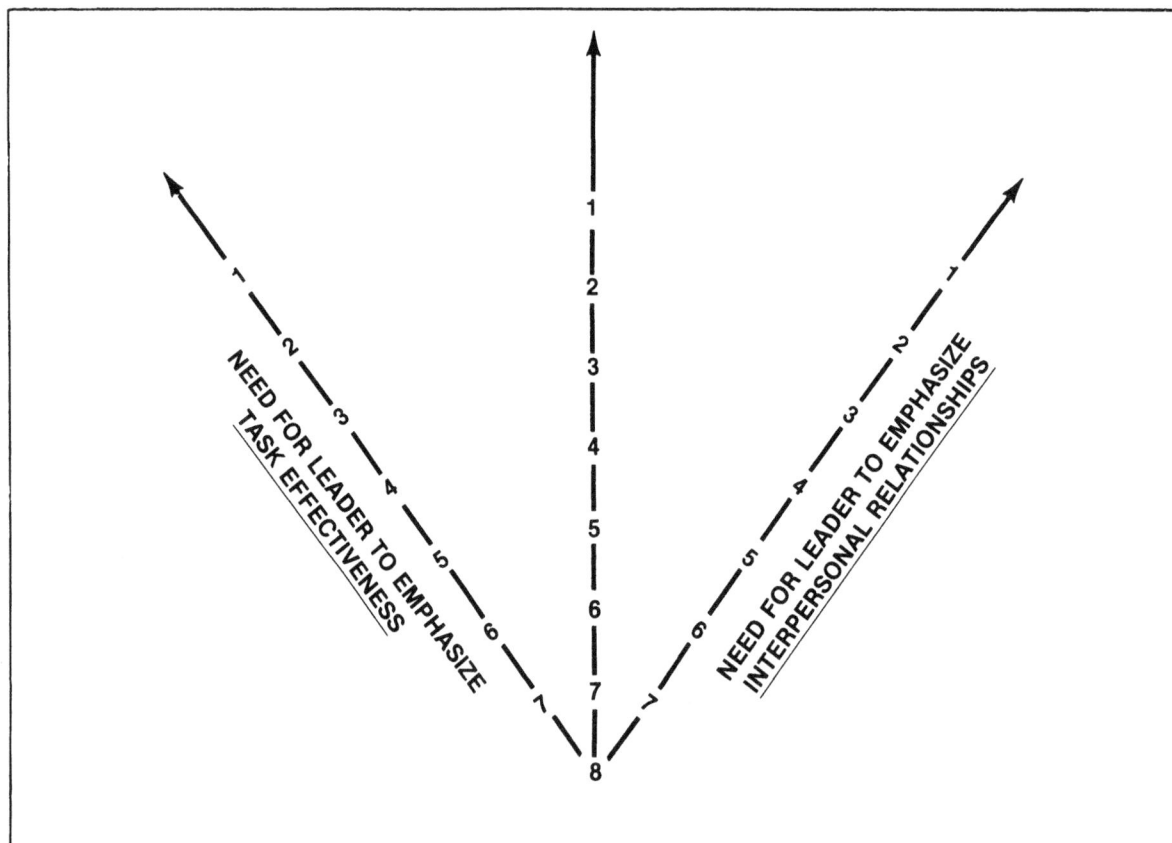

Printed copies of this worksheet are available from the publisher.

- 46 -

DETERMINING THE MOST APPROPRIATE LEADERSHIP STYLE FOR EACH SITUATION

By now you have learned that there are two basic leadership concerns; a concern for relationships and a concern for task effectiveness, and that the degree of emphasis a leader gives to each concern determines his/her leadership style. Figure 4.3, page 31 illustrates a variety of styles which grow out of varying degrees of emphasis a leader may give to the two concerns.

Also, you have learned that there are two basic conditions which combine to determine a group's level of maturity; (the group's willingness and ability to take responsibility for effectively planning and carrying out its work). These conditions are:

1. The quality of interpersonal relationships among group members, and with the leader.

2. The amount of skill and ability the group has which qualifies it to plan and carry out its work, and its commitment to apply these abilities to the task.

Figure 5.1, page 34 illustrates a variety of levels of group maturity.

It is now possible for us to bring together into one diagram all that we have discussed regarding appropriate Leadership styles and Group maturity to illustrate the relationships between these two preeminently important factors, see Figure 5.4, below:

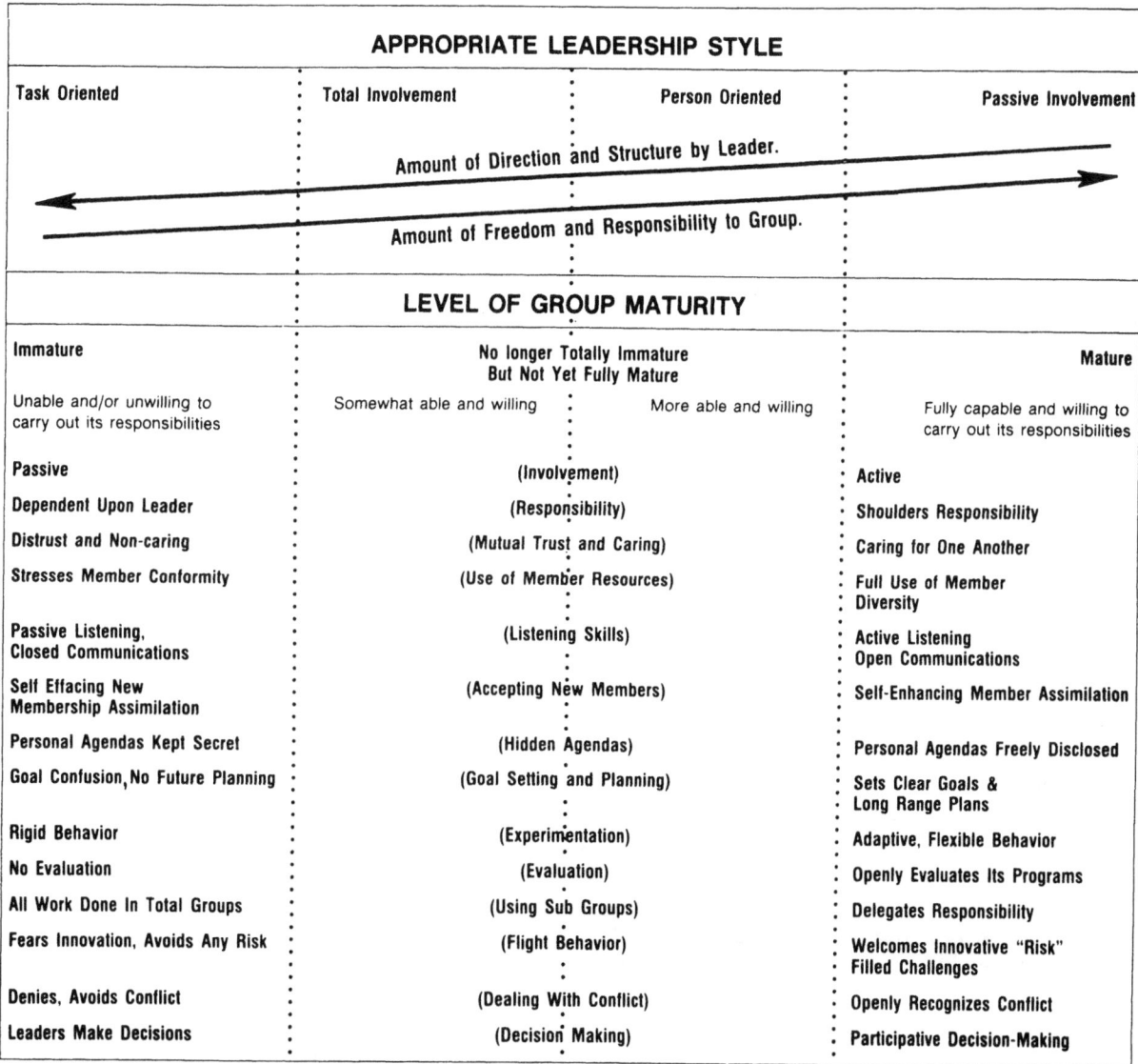

APPROPRIATE LEADERSHIP STYLE			
Task Oriented	Total Involvement	Person Oriented	Passive Involvement

Amount of Direction and Structure by Leader.

Amount of Freedom and Responsibility to Group.

LEVEL OF GROUP MATURITY			
Immature	No longer Totally Immature But Not Yet Fully Mature		Mature
Unable and/or unwilling to carry out its responsibilities	Somewhat able and willing	More able and willing	Fully capable and willing to carry out its responsibilities
Passive	(Involvement)		Active
Dependent Upon Leader	(Responsibility)		Shoulders Responsibility
Distrust and Non-caring	(Mutual Trust and Caring)		Caring for One Another
Stresses Member Conformity	(Use of Member Resources)		Full Use of Member Diversity
Passive Listening, Closed Communications	(Listening Skills)		Active Listening Open Communications
Self Effacing New Membership Assimilation	(Accepting New Members)		Self-Enhancing Member Assimilation
Personal Agendas Kept Secret	(Hidden Agendas)		Personal Agendas Freely Disclosed
Goal Confusion, No Future Planning	(Goal Setting and Planning)		Sets Clear Goals & Long Range Plans
Rigid Behavior	(Experimentation)		Adaptive, Flexible Behavior
No Evaluation	(Evaluation)		Openly Evaluates Its Programs
All Work Done In Total Groups	(Using Sub Groups)		Delegates Responsibility
Fears Innovation, Avoids Any Risk	(Flight Behavior)		Welcomes Innovative "Risk" Filled Challenges
Denies, Avoids Conflict	(Dealing With Conflict)		Openly Recognizes Conflict
Leaders Make Decisions	(Decision Making)		Participative Decision-Making

Figure 5.4

With the exception of the Slave and Martyr behaviors, which are always more-or-less inappropriate, each of the leadership styles are appropriate and effective in certain leadership situations. Therefore, no leadership style is better or worse than the others, per se. There is no "ideal" style which is most appropriate or effective in all situations. Rather, the appropriateness or degree of effectiveness of any style is dependent upon two basic conditions within the group to which leadership is being directed.

It is important to remember that as the level of group task relevant maturity increases or decreases, leadership behavior, in order to remain effective, must be altered accordingly. For example, the appropriate leadership behavior with an immature group is that of placing major emphasis on providing structure to ensure task effectiveness. The appropriate leadership behavior for a fully mature group is that of providing low structure or socio-emotional support since neither is needed to ensure task effectiveness. The leadership style which emphasizes both task effectiveness and relationships; and the one which exhibits high concern for relationships and low concern for task effectiveness, become the appropriate leadership styles as the group progresses from "low" average maturity to "high" average maturity.

It is important to remember that the maturity of a group must be seen in terms of each specific situation or task to be performed. Maturity is defined as the "capacity to set high but attainable goals (achievement-motivation), willingness and ability to take responsibility, education and/or experience of an individual or a group[5]."

A group possessing the willingness and ability to accomplish a specific task without any structure or socio-emotional support being provided by the leader is seen as "above average maturity." The same group may not possess such willingness and ability in another task situation, may need much more structure and direction, and would thus be seen as "average maturity," or below.

MATCHING YOUR LEADERSHIP STYLE TO GROUP NEEDS

There is no single style which is ideal for every situation. Effective leadership, therefore, is not dependent simply upon the styles which the leader utilizes (STYLE RANGE), but also upon the ability of the leader to use the most appropriate style for the group's level of maturity. A leader with a style range of only one or two styles can be effective so long as one works with groups whose level of maturity is such that the styles are appropriate. On the other hand, a leader with a wide style range will be an ineffective leader if one is unsuccessful in utilizing those styles in a manner consistent with the needs of the groups in which leadership is being exercised.

The degree to which you view yourself as being capable of adapting your leadership behavior to most effectively respond to various situations can now be determined by scoring yourself on the following worksheet, **Appropriateness of Your Leadership Behavior.**

The possible responses to each situation have been weighted from 4 to 0, in keeping with the leadership theories discussed earlier. In each situation the style most appropriate for the level of group maturity is weighted 4. The most inappropriate styles are weighted 0. (You will recall the Slave and Martyr styles are always inappropriate, and therefore, are always weighted 0.)

---

[5]Paul Hersey and Kenneth Blanchard, Management of Organizational Behavior, p. 161.

HOW TO DETERMINE APPROPRIATENESS OF YOUR LEADERSHIP BEHAVIOR

There is a difference between your style preferences and range, and the degree to which the style you utilize in a given situation is appropriate, as measured by the effectiveness of that style in that particular situation. FIGURE 5.5 is designed to measure the degree to which you are appropriately using each leadership style.

1. On the FIGURE 5.5, circle the same letter for each situation that you circled on the Figure 2.1, page 16.
2. Find the total numerical values of the letters circled in each leadership style row and enter the figures in the spaces provided for these SCORES.
3. Divide the score given to each leadership style by N = the number of times you selected that style.

4. Round the score up/down at .5 and enter the AVERAGE SCORE for each style in the DEGREE OF APPROPRIATENESS column.

FIGURE 5.5 now provides you important insight into the APPROPRIATENESS of your leadership behavior:

1. The individual DEGREE OF APPROPRIATENESS SCORES tell you the degree to which you are using each style appropriately.
2. The weighting scale used, 0 to 4, is based upon modern leadership theories. The leadership behavior most appropriate for each situation is weighted 4; the least appropriate styles are weighted 0.

Leadership Styles	Situations												Scores	÷	N	=	Degree of Appropriateness
	1	2	3	4	5	6	7	8	9	10	11	12					
TASK ORIENTED	^{1}B	^{1}C	^{3}A	^{4}D	^{1}E	^{1}C	^{2}D	^{4}F	^{1}A	^{2}C	^{2}F	^{4}E					
TOTAL INVOLVEMENT	^{2}D	^{3}F	^{4}C	^{3}A	^{2}C	^{2}B	^{4}E	^{3}B	^{2}F	^{3}A	^{4}E	^{3}D					
PERSON ORIENTED	^{3}A	^{4}D	^{2}B	^{2}F	^{3}B	^{4}D	^{3}A	^{2}E	^{3}C	^{4}E	^{3}C	^{2}F					
PASSIVE INVOLVEMENT	^{4}E	^{2}B	^{1}D	^{1}C	^{4}A	^{3}F	^{1}F	^{1}A	^{4}D	^{1}B	^{1}B	^{1}C					
SLAVE	^{0}C	^{0}A	^{0}E	^{0}E	^{0}F	^{0}E	^{0}B	^{0}D	^{0}B	^{0}F	^{0}D	^{0}A					
MARTYR	^{0}F	^{0}E	^{0}F	^{0}B	^{0}D	^{0}A	^{0}C	^{0}C	^{0}E	^{0}D	^{0}A	^{0}B					

Figure 5.5

The individual APPROPRIATENESS SCORES for each leadership style indicate the degree to which you use each style appropriately, based upon the level of group maturity and the situation.

The twelve situations were constructed to make each of the styles the most appropriate leadership response three out of twelve times (excluding, of course, Slave and Martyr).

A careful study of the scoring indicates, the Person Oriented and Total Involvement styles are "safer" than the Passive Involvement and Task Oriented styles. If a leader has only one or two styles, he/she is "safer" to use these since the margin of possible ineffectiveness is smaller than it is in a situation in which the leader employs a Passive Involvement style with a group needing a Task Oriented leader, or vice versa. It is to be noted that while these styles may be "safer", they are not more appropriate or effective in all situations. In choosing a leadership style there is a difference between being "safe" and being effective.

ADAPTING LEADERSHIP STYLE TO THE SITUATION

In facilitating group maturity the leader must be careful not to reduce task structure and direction and/or socio-emotional support too rapidly. To do so would cause the group to experience a leadership vacuum, in which task effectiveness and relationships may be damaged. The leader must at all times modify his/her style to positively reinforce each new level of group maturity. If the group's maturity level is increasing, this involves reducing task structure and direction while increasing socio-emotional support for the group to accept more responsibility for planning and carrying out its tasks.

A group can regress in maturity as well as progress. If for any reason there is a decline in the level of group maturity, the leader, in order to remain effective, must increase task structure and direction to a level appropriate with the group's new, and lower, level of mature behavior.

Adapting one's leadership style to the group's current level of maturity is the key to appropriate leadership behavior. At times this may require quick and radical shifts in leadership behavior. For example, shifting from a Passive Involvement or Person Oriented style to a Task Oriented style to compensate for a radical regression in group maturity.

It is also true that one's leadership style may influence the maturity level of a group.[1] For example, to help increase a group's maturity level, a leader may delegate a task that he/she is reasonably certain the group can accomplish. After accomplishing the task, the leader gives recognition to the group for the task accomplishment. In addition, the leader may identify other tasks he/she would like to see the group accomplish, all of which help to increase the group's maturity level.

Perhaps three criteria should be considered in determining the appropriate leadership style in any given situation:

1. The group's current situation.

2. The styles of leadership you can utilize (your style range).

3. What makes good sense at the moment.

YOU MAY NOW APPLY YOUR LEARNINGS REGARDING THE RELATIONSHIP OF APPROPRIATE LEADERSHIP STYLES AND GROUP MATURITY BY COMPLETING THE FOLLOWING WORKSHEETS, STEP 6.

---

[1] See Paul Hersey and Kenneth Blanchard, *Management of Organizational Behavior*, pp. 201-206.

WORKSHEETS
for
Applying Your Learnings to
the Survey Situations
Group Needs

Each of the twelve situations in the SURVEY give you some information about the level of group maturity, the current leadership style being utilized, and the results of that style in the situation. From this you should be able to select the most appropriate leadership behavior for the new situation.

The worksheets are intended to help you gain skill in analyzing a group and its situation to determine the most appropriate leadership style.

Please complete the worksheets, attempting to utilize the insights into effective leadership behavior you have now gained. As you complete each situation, you are encouraged to thoroughly study the page given to that particular situation in Step 7. This will allow you to compare your responses to those of the author and to gain insight into the possible results of each leadership style in that situation. Then return to the next situation in Step 6.

SITUATION NO. 1: *(Example)*

YOU HAVE BEEN PROVIDING THE GROUP WITH SOCIO-EMOTIONAL SUPPORT, BUT LITTLE DIRECTION. RELATIONSHIPS AND EFFECTIVENESS ARE VERY GOOD. MEMBERS HAVE SUGGESTIONS FOR NEEDED PROGRAM CHANGES.

Diagnosis:

1. Group maturity: _____**Above average**_____

2. Current leadership style:_____**Person Oriented**_____

3. Most appropriate leadership style for new situation: _____**Passive Involvement**_____

_____

SITUATION NO. 2:

YOUR HIGHLY EFFECTIVE GROUP HAS BEEN ALMOST ENTIRELY SELF-DIRECTED. NOW, HOWEVER, IT IS HAVING DIFFICULTY CARRYING OUT ITS PRESENT ASSIGNMENT.

Diagnosis:

1. Group maturity: _____

2. Current leadership style: _____

3. Most appropriate leadership style for new situation: _____

_____

SITUATION NO. 3:

YOU HAVE BEEN FRIENDLY AND SUPPORTIVE OF THE GROUP'S GOALS AND IDEAS. RELATIONSHIPS ARE GOOD; HOWEVER, USUAL EFFECTIVENESS IS BEGINNING TO DECLINE.

Diagnosis:

1. Group maturity: _____

2. Current leadership style: _____

3. Most appropriate leadership style for new situation: _____

_____

SITUATION NO. 4:

YOU ARE THE NEW LEADER OF A VERY INEFFECTIVE GROUP. THERE IS MUCH TASK CONFUSION AND RELATIONSHIPS ARE POOR. THE PREVIOUS LEADER WAS UNINVOLVED IN THE GROUP'S AFFAIRS.

Diagnosis:

1. Group maturity: _____

2. Previous leadership style: _____

3. Most appropriate leadership style for new situation: _____

   _____

SITUATION NO. 5:

YOUR GROUP HAS JUST COMPLETED A LONG-RANGE PLANNING PROCESS AND IS NOW READY TO PUT THEIR PLANS INTO ACTION. YOU WERE ALMOST ENTIRELY UNINVOLVED IN THE PLANNING.

Diagnosis:

1. Group maturity: _____

2. Current leadership style: _____

3. Most appropriate leadership style for new situation: _____

   _____

SITUATION NO. 6:

THE GROUP HAS GROWN TO BE QUITE EFFECTIVE AND RELATIONSHIPS ARE GOOD. YOU HAVE BEEN PROVIDING SOCIO-EMOTIONAL SUPPORT, BUT FEEL YOU MAY NOT BE GIVING THE GROUP AS MUCH DIRECTION AS YOU SHOULD.

Diagnosis:

1. Group maturity: _____

2. Current leadership style: _____

3. Most appropriate leadership style for new situation: _____

   _____

SITUATION NO. 7:

RELATIONSHIPS AND EFFECTIVENESS ARE IMPROVING STEADILY. YOU HAVE BEEN INTER-
PRETING THE TASK AND GIVING EXPLICIT INSTRUCTIONS FOR CARRYING IT OUT.

Diagnosis:

1. Group maturity: _____

2. Current leadership style: _____

3. Most appropriate leadership style for new situation: _____

_____

SITUATION NO. 8:

PREVIOUS GROUP RELATIONSHIPS AND EFFECTIVENESS WERE POOR. BY GIVING CLEAR
ASSIGNMENTS AND CHECKING ON FOLLOW-THROUGH, BOTH ARE IMPROVING. NOW, HOW-
EVER, THE GROUP IS CONFUSED OVER A REQUIREMENT TO SUBMIT A 20% REDUCED BUDGET
WITHIN TWO WEEKS.

Diagnosis:

1. Group maturity: _____

2. Current leadership style: _____

3. Most appropriate leadership style for new situation: _____

_____

SITUATION NO. 9:

YOU HAVE JUST BEEN APPONTED THE LEADER OF A GROUP WITH AN EXCELLENT RECORD OF
EFFECTIVENESS AND RELATIONSHIPS. THE PREVIOUS LEADER WAS RELATIVELY UNINVOLVED
IN GROUP AFFAIRS.

Diagnosis:

1. Group maturity: _____

2. Previous leadership style: _____

3. Most appropriate leadership style for new situation: _____

_____

SITUATION NO. 10:

YOUR GROUP HAS A LONG RECORD OF EFFECTIVENESS. INTERPERSONAL RELATIONSHIPS HAVE BEEN GOOD. IT HAS NOT BEEN NECESSARY FOR YOU TO BE CONCERNED ABOUT GIVING SUPPORT OR DIRECTION. NOW, SERIOUS CONFLICT HAS DEVELOPED WITHIN THE GROUP. DIFFERING MEMBERS HAVE BROKEN OFF RELATIONSHIPS.

Diagnosis:

1. Group maturity: _____

2. Current leadership style: _____

3. Most appropriate leadership style for new situation: _____

   _____

SITUATION NO. 11:

YOU HAVE BEEN GIVING EXPLICIT INSTRUCTIONS AND CHECKING ON FOLLOW-THROUGH. THE GROUP HAS GROWN IN MATURITY. NOW, HOWEVER, EFFECTIVENESS IS DECLINING AND MEMBERS SEEM TO BE QUESTIONING YOUR AUTHORITARIAN LEADERSHIP.

Diagnosis:

1. Group maturity: _____

2. Current leadership style: _____

3. Most appropriate leadership style for new situation: _____

   _____

SITUATION NO. 12:

YOUR GROUP HAS SEVERAL NEWLY APPOINTED WILLING, BUT INEXPERIENCED, MEMBERS. YOU MUST NOW INSTALL NEW ORGANIZATIONAL POLICIES.

Diagnosis:

1. Group maturity: _____

2. Current leadership style:_____ **(not indicated)**_____

3. Most appropriate leadership style for new situation: _____

   _____

REFLECTING ON
YOUR RESPONSES TO
THE TWELVE SITUATIONS

SITUATION NO. 1:

YOU HAVE BEEN PROVIDING THE GROUP WITH SOCIO-EMOTIONAL SUPPORT, BUT LITTLE DIRECTION. RELATIONSHIPS AND EFFECTIVENESS ARE VERY GOOD. MEMBERS HAVE SUGGESTIONS FOR NEEDED PROGRAM CHANGES.

Diagnosis:

1. Group maturity: **Above average**

2. Current leadership style: **Person Oriented**

3. Your chosen style of leadership for new situation:

E. Passive Involvement: Allow the group to plan and implement the change on its own.

(4) The group has grown to an above average group under the Person Oriented style. You should be considering a change to reinforce this growth. Now with the need for change, and the obvious interest of the group in planning its implementation, you have a good opportunity to reinforce their growth by giving them greater responsibility in a major issue.

A. Person Oriented: Allow the group to plan the change, remaining available for consultation.

(3) This is no change from your current style, and while it would maintain relationships and ensure effectiveness, it would not facilitate further group maturity.

D. Total Involvement: Implement necessary changes, incorporating group recommendations.

(2) This may get the change implemented; however, it would not reinforce the group maturity already achieved. Effectiveness may decline.

B. Task Oriented: Plan the change and assign responsibilities for carrying it out.

(1) Inappropriate with this group of above average maturity. Could damage relationships. Effectiveness would decline sharply.

C. Slave: Allow the group to plan the change, then carry it out for them.

(0) While reinforcing group growth during the planning stage, it would reverse the growth during implementation. The group would be unsure of your role and your opinion of their abilities. Effectiveness during the implementation would decline sharply.

F. Martyr: Instruct the group that no program is ever perfect and present specific strategy; assigning responsibilities for implementation.

(0) This inappropriate style would be expected to damage relationships and send effectiveness into a downward plunge.

SITUATION NO. 2:

YOUR HIGHLY EFFECTIVE GROUP HAS BEEN ALMOST ENTIRELY SELF-DIRECTED. NOW, HOWEVER, IT IS HAVING DIFFICULTY CARRYING OUT ITS PRESENT ASSIGNMENT.

Diagnosis:

1. Group maturity: **Above average**

2. Current leadership style: **Passive Involvement**

3. Your chosen style of leadership for new situation:

D. Person Oriented: Encourage the group to continue working on the assignment, remaining available for consultation.

(4)   Providing some structure for communication and moral support is necessary to enable this group, above average in maturity and effectiveness, to stretch their capabilities in handling this tougher than average assignment. This approach would give the group the support it needs, while also allowing the group to find its own solution.

F. Total Involvement: Give instructions for carrying out the assignment, incorporating group suggestions.

(3)   While this approach would work, it might create an unnecessary dependency upon you to provide structure and direction in future tough situations. Group maturity would be hindered in such instances.

B. Passive Involvement: Leave the group free to work it out as they see fit.

(2)   This is no change in your leadership style and is no longer effective, since the group could not handle this assignment without your support.

C. Task Oriented: Give specific step-by-step instructions for carrying out the assignment.

(1)   This provides more structure and direction than the situation calls for and would, no doubt, be experienced by the group as a lack of confidence in their ability. Relationships would suffer and effectiveness would decline.

A. Slave: Carry out the assignment for them.

(0)   Your doing their work would cause unhealthy dependency, hostility, or both. Effectiveness would sharply decline. Relationships would be damaged.

E. Martyr: Decide what has gone wrong with the group to cause this sudden ineffectiveness, and correct it.

(0)   Nothing has gone wrong with the group. The problem is in the situation, not in the group. This approach would damage relationships and block effectiveness.

SITUATION NO. 3:

YOU HAVE BEEN FRIENDLY AND SUPPORTIVE OF THE GROUP'S GOALS AND IDEAS. RELATIONSHIPS ARE GOOD; HOWEVER, USUAL EFFECTIVENESS IS BEGINNING TO DECLINE.

Diagnosis:

1. Group maturity: **Average**

2. Current leadership style: **Person Oriented**

3. Your chosen style of leadership for new situation:

C. Total Involvement: Share your observations with the group, inviting suggestions for improving effectiveness.

(4) Your group, of average maturity, has until recently been effective under your Person Oriented style of leadership. The present decline indicates a need for a bit more structure and direction. This can best be accomplished with a group of average maturity and effectiveness, when relationships are good, by involving them in deciding how much direction is needed and how you will give it.

A. Task Oriented: Present new procedures, emphasizing the need for following them closely.

(3) The amount of structure and direction given would be more than necessary for a group of average maturity, and could possibly damage relationships, retard group maturity, or both.

B. Person Oriented: Encourage the group to formulate plans for improving effectiveness, remaining available for consultation.

(2) This is no change from your current style and, while maintaining good relationships, could be expected to result in a continuing decline in effectiveness.

D. Passive Involvement: Do nothing until it became clear whether effectiveness would improve or continue to decline.

(1) Effectiveness is already suffering from a lack of structure and direction. This response would result in even less structure and direction, increase ineffectiveness, and may tend to cause tensions in the relationships.

E. Slave: Do more of the group's work yourself.

(0) This response may maintain the relationship, but would retard group maturity and effectiveness by not providing necessary structure and direction, and would foster inappropriate dependency upon your leadership.

F. Martyr: Specify and enforce procedures. Do much of the work yourself.

(0) This controlling approach would be inappropriate with a group of average maturity which, until recently, had maintained average effectiveness, and would no doubt damage the relationship as well as significantly increase ineffectiveness.

SITUATION NO. 4:

YOU ARE THE NEW LEADER OF A VERY INEFFECTIVE GROUP. THERE IS MUCH TASK CONFUSION AND RELATIONSHIPS ARE POOR. THE PREVIOUS LEADER WAS UNINVOLVED IN THE GROUP'S AFFAIRS.

Diagnosis:

1. Group maturity: **Below average**

2. Previous leadership style: **Passive Involvement**

3. Your chosen style of leadership for new situation:

D. Task Oriented: Define the task, give specific assignments, and check on follow-through.

(4)   This immature group is suffering so much from a lack of sufficient structure and direction it cannot function at all. An approach that puts emphasis on task orientation is needed to give the group a sense of purpose and direction.

A. Total Involvement: Begin providing more structure and direction, encouraging group recommendations.

(3)   This should help establish relationships, but only temporarily since the group will soon become frustrated and ashamed at their inability to add anything constructive to the planning.

F. Person Oriented: Encourage the group to formulate plans for improving effectiveness, remaining available for consultation.

(2)   This would do no more than further frustrate the group, since this immature group would be unable to formulate plans for improving effectiveness.

C. Passive Involvement: Allow the group to chart its own course.

(1)   This is no change from the previous leader's style, which has proven to be ineffective.

E. Slave: Do the group's work yourself.

(0)   This approach would confuse the group even more and generate inappropriate dependency. Relationships and effectiveness, already poor, would degenerate even more.

B. Martyr: Do the group's work yourself until you were able to find out what is wrong with the group, and correct it.

(0)   This is inappropriate since the problem is in the style of the previous leader, and not in the group. Hostility would be generated and ineffectiveness would continue. Members could be expected to remove themselves from the group.

SITUATION NO. 5:

YOUR GROUP HAS JUST COMPLETED A LONG-RANGE PLANNING PROCESS AND IS NOW READY TO PUT THEIR PLANS INTO ACTION. YOU WERE ALMOST ENTIRELY UNINVOLVED IN THE PLANNING.

Diagnosis:

1. Group maturity: **Above average**

2. Current leadership style: **Passive Involvement**

3. Your chosen style of leadership for new situation:

A. Passive Involvement: Allow the group to implement plans on its own.

(4) This approach best allows the group to continue its development by providing its own direction and support for implementing its plans.

B. Person Oriented: Encourage the group to implement its plans, remaining available for consultation.

(3) This should be effective for implementation; however, it does not fully reflect the group's maturity and may run the risk of developing a tendency of turning to you for advice too quickly when difficulties are encountered.

C. Total Involvement: Initiate and direct implementation procedures, incorporating group recommendations.

(2) This would provide more structure and control than this group needs. Relationships may be damaged. Maturity and effectiveness would decline.

E. Task Oriented: Implement the plans by defining roles and assigning responsibilities.

(1) An inappropriate approach with a group which has demonstrated its ability to provide its own structure and direction. Conflict would erupt and effectiveness would decline.

F. Slave: Wait until the group has formulated implementation procedures, then do whatever you could to carry them out.

(0) Your intervening to do work which the group is capable of performing denies members a chance for further maturity and achievement. Relationships and effectiveness would sharply decline.

D. Martyr: Remind them that most groups make plans, but few ever carry them out. Give specific implementation procedures, doing everything you could personally to carry them out.

(0) This reflects an insensitivity on your part to the maturity of the group. This group has already proven it is not like "most groups." There is at this point no reason to suspect they may not follow-through on their plans. Relationships and effectiveness would sharply decline.

SITUATION NO. 6:

THE GROUP HAS GROWN TO BE QUITE EFFECTIVE AND RELATIONSHIPS ARE GOOD. YOU HAVE BEEN PROVIDING SOCIO-EMOTIONAL SUPPORT, BUT FEEL YOU MAY NOT BE GIVING THE GROUP AS MUCH DIRECTION AS YOU SHOULD.

Diagnosis:

1. Group maturity: **Average**

2. Current leadership style: **Person Oriented:**

3. Your chosen style of leadership for new situation:

D. Person Oriented: Continue to play a friendly supportive role.

(4) The group is in transition and you are now questioning your leadership behavior. You could begin to provide more structure, but the group's maturity and effectiveness does not warrant this. You could become less involved; however, this "newly average" group still needs the security of your support and consultation. Your best bet would be to continue your present style.

F. Passive Involvement: Leave the group free to provide for its own support and direction.

(3) The group would probably experience this withdrawal as a loss of interest in their welfare and task. Relationships would be strained somewhat, and effectiveness growth would be slowed down or stopped altogether.

B. Total Involvement: Discuss your feelings with the group and begin to provide more structure and direction.

(2) This would not reflect the group's new maturity and effectiveness; and therefore would be inappropriate. The group's maturity and effectiveness would decline.

C. Task Oriented: Exercise more control by specifying procedures and responsibilities.

(1) This would be in direct opposition to the growth of the group. Group morale and effectiveness would sharply decline.

E. Slave: Begin doing as much of their detail work as you could.

(0) This would provide far less structure and support than is needed by an average group, and deny them opportunities for implementing their own decisions. Group maturity and effectiveness would sharply decline and relationships would be damaged.

A. Martyr: Inform the group you are feeling guilty about your lack of involvement and begin to exercise control of decision-making and assignments.

(0) This is an attempt to control by guilt, to bring the group into subjection by making them feel guilty for having left you outside of their affairs. It would provide an inappropriate amount of structure and control, sending relationships and effectiveness into a tail-spin.

SITUATION NO. 7:

RELATIONSHIPS AND EFFECTIVENESS ARE IMPROVING STEADILY. YOU HAVE BEEN INTERPRETING THE TASK AND GIVING EXPLICIT INSTRUCTIONS FOR CARRYING IT OUT.

Diagnosis:

1. Group maturity: **(Low) average**

2. Current leadership style: **Task Oriented**

3. Your chosen style of leadership for new situation:

E. Total Involvement: Continue to press for increased effectiveness while allowing the group more say in defining and planning the task.

(4) The group has matured under your controlling style of leadership. This growth pattern would now be best facilitated by a leadership style which provides less control, but enough to maintain a sense of direction; while at the same time recognizing the maturity which has occurred by allowing the group a greater say in how they want to carry out their task.

A. Person Oriented: Turn planning and decision-making over to the group, remaining available for consultation.

(3) This approach may make the group feel more important and involved; however, it runs the risk of creating a perceived vacuum of leadership and a loss of sufficient structure to facilitate increased effectiveness.

D. Task Oriented: Emphasize the importance of their work and have other assignments laid out when current tasks are completed.

(2) This would be no change from your current style. With no increased opportunity to assume more responsibility, the group's maturity and effectiveness would level off and, if you persist in this style, begin to decline.

F. Passive Involvement: Allow the group to chart its own course.

(1) This would place inappropriate responsibilities on this group of low average maturity, and no doubt would be experienced as a loss of interest or sense of direction on your part. Effectiveness would decline.

B. Slave: Do as much of the group's work as possible.

(0) This inappropriate approach would cause a leadership "vacuum," a loss of sense of direction, and foster dependency of members upon yourself. Maturity and effectiveness would decline sharply.

C. Martyr: Remind the group it is still far from perfect. Outline specific steps for improvement and work harder yourself.

(0) This approach would cause the group to feel guilty about the level of effectiveness not yet attained, rather than give positive reinforcement for the gains already made. The group would either become angry with you or more dependent upon you. Maturity and effectiveness would decline sharply.

SITUATION NO. 8:

PREVIOUS GROUP RELATIONSHIPS AND EFFECTIVENESS WERE POOR. BY GIVING CLEAR ASSIGNMENTS AND CHECKING ON FOLLOW-THROUGH, BOTH ARE IMPROVING. NOW, HOWEVER, THE GROUP IS CONFUSED OVER A REQUIREMENT TO SUBMIT A 20% REDUCED BUDGET WITHIN TWO WEEKS.

Diagnosis:

1. Group maturity: **Below average**

2. Current leadership style: **Task Oriented**

3. Your chosen style of leadership for new situation:

___

F. Task Oriented: Define the task and give explicit steps for carrying it out.

(4) Though developing, this group is still below average as evidenced by their reaction to the new situation. The group has been responding satisfactorily to your Task Oriented style. Your best choice here would be to continue providing structure and direction.

B. Total Involvement: Implement necessary procedures, incorporating group recommendations.

(3) At present this group is not demonstrating the degree of maturity necessary to do the necessary planning in the time allowed, unless you give more structure than the Total Involvement style would provide.

E. Person Oriented: Encourage the group to revise its budget, being careful not to hurt leader-member relationships.

(2) This inappropriate approach would not get the job done in the short time allowed, and would reinforce the group's present state of confusion. Newly gained effectiveness and maturity would be lost.

A. Passive Involvement: Leave the group alone to do the necessary budget planning.

(1) Time deadlines would not be met. Confusion would increase dramatically. Maturity and effectiveness would plunge downward.

D. Slave: Prepare the new budget for them.

(0) This would ensure the deadline being met; however, would do nothing to further develop the group's potential. The group would have lost a valuable learning experience, and an inappropriate dependency upon you as leader would have been developed.

C. Martyr: Inform the group you are as confused as they, and prepare the budget for them.

(0) Time deadlines would be met; however, the group would have lost a learning experience and developed inappropriate dependency upon a "confused" leader who goes ahead and plans without them. Maturity and effectiveness would plunge downward.

SITUATION NO. 9:

YOU HAVE JUST BEEN APPOINTED THE LEADER OF A GROUP WITH AN EXCELLENT RECORD OF EFFECTIVENESS AND RELATIONSHIPS. THE PREVIOUS LEADER WAS RELATIVELY UNINVOLVED IN GROUP AFFAIRS.

Diagnosis:

1. Group maturity: **Above average**

2. Previous leadership style: **Passive Involvement**

3. Your chosen style of leadership for new situation:

D. Passive Involvement: Allow the group to function as before.

(4)   Under the previous leader's Passive Involvement the group has developed above average capabilities, and relationships are good. Your best choice would be to reflect that maturity by continuing with that style.

C. Person Oriented: Encourage the group to continue operating as previously, being careful not to damage new leader-group relationships.

(3)   This should be effective for establishing relationships; however, it would not fully reflect the group's level of maturity.

F. Total Involvement: Talk it over with the group, then assign new roles and responsibilities.

(2)   An inappropriate approach to an already very effective group, whose present structures are working very well. Time would be wasted and effectiveness would decline.

A. Task Oriented: Define new roles and responsibilities, and make specific assignments.

(1)   This approach would not reinforce the group's maturity and effectiveness. Relationships would be damaged. Group effectiveness would decline.

B. Slave: Do all of the group's work you possibly could.

(0)   This would give the appearance that you have no confidence in their capabilities, an inappropriate way to establish relationships with an effective group.

E. Martyr: Inform them you feel unworthy to lead such an effective group, and ask for full support. Assign new roles and responsibilities.

(0)   This would be an attempt to gain control through pity. The group would have to choose between rejecting you as leader, or sacrifice much of their effectiveness and maturity.

SITUATION NO. 10:

YOUR GROUP HAS A LONG RECORD OF EFFECTIVENESS. INTERPERSONAL RELATIONSHIPS HAVE BEEN GOOD. IT HAS NOT BEEN NECESSARY FOR YOU TO BE CONCERNED ABOUT GIVING SUPPORT OR DIRECTION. NOW, SERIOUS CONFLICT HAS DEVELOPED WITHIN THE GROUP. DIFFERING MEMBERS HAVE BROKEN OFF RELATIONSHIPS.

Diagnosis:

1. Group maturity: **Above average**

2. Current leadership style: **Passive Involvement**

3. Your chosen style of leadership for new situation:

_____

E. Person Oriented: Encourage members to resolve the conflict, being careful not to hurt leader-member relationships.

(4) This approach is the most appropriate because of the serious nature of the conflict. The group possesses the skills and maturity to manage the conflict; however, support is needed from you to initiate relationships again.

A. Total Involvement: Bring the group together and suggest a solution to the conflict

(3) This would be appropriate only if the Person Oriented style did not prove successful in managing the conflict.

C. Task Oriented: Impose rules for resolving the conflict, and check on follow-through.

(2) This approach would be inappropriate for a group of this maturity. Relationships and effectiveness would be further damaged.

B. Passive Involvement: Do nothing.

(1) This approach, though normally the most appropriate for this group, even in conflict, would be inappropriate where relationships have broken off completely. Restoring communication would be a necessary precondition to satisfactorily managing the conflict.

F. Slave: Ask the differing sides what you might do to correct the problem, and do what they suggest.

(0) Inappropriate and dangerous. The differing parties can and should settle the differences. Your attempts to please everyone, without their face-to-face involvement, would not reflect the group's maturity. Relationships may be irreparably damaged. Maturity and effectiveness would decline sharply.

D. Martyr: Inform the group such behavior is immature. Outline specific steps for resolving the conflict.

(0) This would be an attempt to dictate the resolution and to bring the differing parties to accept it because of guilt, and would be most inappropriate for a group of this maturity. It would generate hostilities, further damage relationships, and send effectiveness into a downward plunge.

SITUATION NO. 11:

YOU HAVE BEEN GIVING EXPLICIT INSTRUCTIONS AND CHECKING ON FOLLOW-THROUGH. THE GROUP HAS GROWN IN MATURITY. NOW, HOWEVER, EFFECTIVENESS IS DECLINING AND MEMBERS SEEM TO BE QUESTIONING YOUR AUTHORITARIAN LEADERSHIP.

Diagnosis:

1. Group maturity: **(Low) average**

2. Current leadership style: **Task Oriented**

3. Your chosen style of leadership for new situation:

E. Total Involvement: Give less explicit instructions, but continue to check on follow-through.

(4) The group has achieved a new level of maturity and effectiveness, but your leadership has not changed to reflect this. Since you have not reinforced their new level, the group is beginning to regress. A Total Involvement approach, while a little late in coming, should reverse this downward trend.

C. Person Oriented: Encourage the group to assume more responsibility for its affairs. Remain available for consultation.

(3) This would reflect a greater degree of maturity than has been achieved, and effectiveness could be expected to continue declining.

F. Task Oriented: Emphasize the importance of the task, and give specific assignments. Check on follow-through.

(2) This is no change from your current style. Group maturity and effectiveness could be expected to continue declining and level off at below average. Relationships would be damaged.

B. Passive Involvement: Allow the group to function on its own.

(1) This is an inappropriate approach with a group of low average maturity whose effectiveness is already declining. It would be experienced as a leadership vacuum. Effectiveness and relationships would decline sharply.

D. Slave: Personally take care of important tasks.

(0) While this approach may improve relationships for a while, it would send group maturity and effectiveness into a downward plunge.

A. Martyr: Let the group know your disappointment regarding their attitude, and set a good example by doing all the work you possibly could.

(0) The group is already showing signs of too much control. This approach of "rule by guilt" would only cause hostility and send effectiveness into a tail-spin.

SITUATION NO. 12:

YOUR GROUP HAS SEVERAL NEWLY APPOINTED WILLING, BUT INEXPERIENCED, MEMBERS. YOU MUST NOW INSTALL NEW ORGANIZATIONAL POLICIES.

Diagnosis:

1. Group maturity: **Below average**

2. Current leadership style: **Not indicated**

3. Your chosen style of leadership for new situation:

E. Task Oriented: Define the task, assign specific roles and responsibilities, and check on follow-through.

(4) Group members are new and inexperienced, and have had little time to develop relationships. Your best choice is to provide structure and direction until the group begins to mature, which may be soon, since the group wants to work.

D. Total Involvement: Incorporate group recommendations into your plans for initiating new policies.

(3) This group does not possess the degree of maturity, and has not had opportunity to demonstrate the effectiveness which would make this the most appropriate approach.

F. Person Oriented: Encourage the group to define its task and to assign roles and responsibilities, being careful not to hurt leader-member relationships.

(2) This would not provide the amount of structure and direction needed to ensure group development. Confusion would set in. Developing relationships and effectiveness would be negatively effected.

C. Passive Involvement: Allow the group to implement policies on its own.

(1) This would create a leadership vacuum. Group morale would suffer greatly. Relationships and effectiveness would be severely retarded, or destroyed.

A. Slave: Inform the group your role is to serve them. Demonstrate this by implementing new policies on your own.

(0) This approach would deny the members a chance for involvement and growth. Under such an approach maturity and effectiveness could never happen.

B. Martyr: Inform them the new policies are complex and, to make it easier for them, you would assign their roles and responsibilities and do most of the work yourself.

(0) This is an attempt to control by convincing the members the work is too difficult for them. This would send motivation and developing maturity into a tail-spin.

CONCLUSION

Having now studied the theories upon which "A Survey of Your Leadership Styles" is based, you may wish to take the survey again to determine the degree of new learnings you have achieved.

"A Survey of Your Leadership Styles" has given you your own perceptions of your leadership behavior. The groups with whom you work may perceive you the same, or quite differently. You can determine the degree of similarity between your perception, and the group's perception, by having group members complete *How You Can Be A More Effective Leader: A Self-Analysis Tool.*[1]

You are encouraged to continue your studies in leadership by reading the following materials.[2]

1. Norman Shawchuck. *What it Means To Be a Church Leader: A Biblical Point of View.* (Leith, ND: Spiritual Growth Resources, 1984).

2. Norman Shawchuck and Roger Heuser. *Leading the Congregation: Caring for Yourself While Serving the People.* (Nashville: Abingdon Press, 1993).

3. Norman Shawchuck and Roger Heuser. *Managing the Congregation.* (Nashville: Abingdon Press, 1995).

4. Norman Shawchuck and Rueben Job. *A Guide to Prayer for Ministers and Other Servants.* (Nashville: The Upper Room, 1983).

5. Norman Shawchuck and Gustave Rath. *Benchmarks of Quality in the Church: 21 Ways to Continuously Improve the Content of Your Ministry.* (Nashville: Abingdon Press, 1994)

---

[1] The instrument was prepared by Norman Shawchuck, Ph.D., and may be ordered from Spiritual Growth Resources.

[2] All of the books may be ordered from Spiritual Growth Resources, Leith, ND. 58529, 1-800-359-7363.

APPENDIX:
POSITIVE AND NEGATIVE EXPRESSIONS OF THE LEADERSHIP STYLES

In 1993 - 94, I worked with a team of civilian and military personnel offering leadership training to the US Navy, Coast Guard and Marine chaplains around the world. During a session on situational leadership, one group said to me, "The terms "maximum" and "minimum" (e.g., Fig. 4.3, p.31) sound too pejorative. No chaplain wants to be seen as having minimum concern for ministry effectiveness, or for interpersonal relationships. So everyone wants to be Total Involvement all the time." My response to the group's concerns is given below -- translated into non-military language.

The terms, minimum or maximum concern for relationships or for ministry, are not intended to be pejorative but to accentuate the differing degrees of emphasis a leader may put upon each of the leadership styles. For example, a leader may prefer a Person Oriented style above all the others. This means that, in leadership situations, she/he demonstrates a greater concern for interpersonal relationships, and a lesser concern for ministry effectiveness.

I think no one comes into the ministry as a Passive person. But there is a process in many religious systems (judicatories and congregations) that makes some pastors to become passive. The organization shapes the leader more than the leader shapes the organization. This is true of all organizations.

Nonetheless, there are two real possibilities within each style, either of which a pastor may adopt. One possibility is more negative, and the other more positive. I will give some brief examples of the more positive and negative expressions of each style.

PASSIVE INVOLVEMENT:

A. I don't care:
I don't intend to stay here very long. I want to get a bigger church. So, I play the political game, and the "Good old boy" system to stay on the good side of the bishop and the other church officials. My motto is, make no waves.

Most of the people in my congregation come to church so seldom that I hardly get to know them. They don't seem to like me, so I don't do much visiting. If they need me, they know where to find me.

B. I do care:
The growth and ministry results of this church are very important to me. However, I think the leaders in the congregation are fully capable of planning and implementing the ministry on their own. If I leave them alone they will grow in their ministry effectiveness, and in their ability to take responsibility for the quality of life in the congregation.

PERSON ORIENTED:

A. I don't care:
I don't care much about all the work that goes on around here, and I leave it to others. I was called by God to be with people, and to minister to people. Caring for people is what my ministry is about. I leave the rest to others.

The people I serve are so brittle and immature that if I were to correct them, or instruct them to do better, they would break like crystal. Therefore, I find it best to treat them with 'kid gloves,' and not to emphasize mission or ministry. (NOTE: These leaders store up resentment within themselves --ultimately becoming bitter and cynical persons. They suffer from pent up hostilities and disappointments. They become "old bears" not "teddy bears.")

B. **I do care:**
I care a great deal about the ministry of this congregation, and I honestly feel the volunteers can do it well. So, I give them full responsibility. However, when they ask for assistance or encouragement I give it to them. I believe that if I create a safe and accepting environment, they will do the work on their own -- and become even more capable to take on larger tasks.

TASK ORIENTED:

A. **I don't care:**
These volunteers are not equipped to much of anything -- and the paid personnel aren't much better. I can not trust them to do anything right unless I lay it out for them -- and then check up to be sure they are doing it right.

B. **I do care:**
Most of our volunteer workers are new to their ministry assignments, and are unable to carry out a task without clear supervision. However, I know they are willing to learn, and they relate well with one another. My job here is to lay out clear tasks and guidelines, and then show them how to do it. If I do this they will become more capable of assuming new responsibilities in the future.

TOTAL INVOLVEMENT:

A. **I care, but I have to keep a hand on the control:**
These ministry leaders want more freedom to plan and carry out the ministry without my supervision. But I don't trust them to do a good job. So I have to stay involved. I attend all the committee meetings, and allow no plan or program to go forward without my review and approval.

B. **I do care:**
The staff and volunteers who carry out our ministry programs are doing well. I see new growth occurring. They are capable of doing good work. They don't need me to bail them out of problems. But they do need me to be there -- and to be fully involved, as one of them. My role is to inspire them by my participation, and to model good relationships and work behavior.

Notes

Notes

Notes

Notes

Notes

Notes

www.ingramcontent.com/pod-product-compliance
Lightning Source LLC
LaVergne TN
LVHW081320060426

835509LV00015B/1608